neopets®

The OFFICIAL COOKBOOK

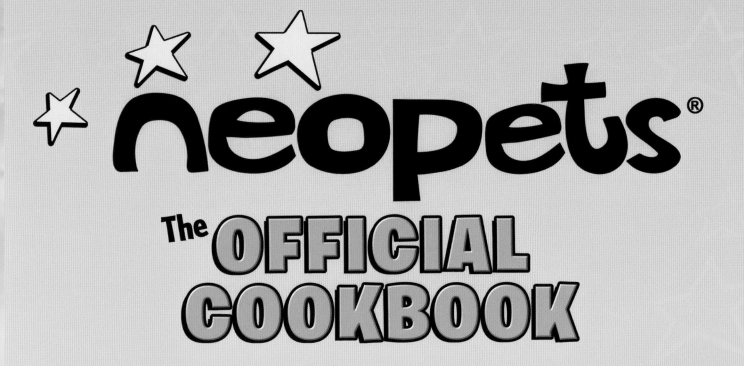

neopets®

The OFFICIAL COOKBOOK

Recipes by **Rebecca Woods**

Words by **Erinn Pascal**

Andrews McMeel
PUBLISHING®

CONTENTS

DIETARY SYMBOLS

Not everyone is a Grarrl or a Skeith, meaning they eat anything and everything. Look out for these symbols throughout the book to make the recipes work for you.

 Suitable for
VEGETARIANS

 Suitable for
VEGANS

 Suitable for those on a
GLUTEN-FREE DIET

A WORD ON SPELLINGS

Neopets was created in England by **Adam Powell** and **Donna Williams** in the late 1990s. As such, many of the foods in this cookbook are spelled the British way, i.e., *omelettes* instead of *omelets*. To preserve the Neopian spellings, this book goes by the website's spellings for recipe names as well as italicized item descriptions. It also includes both metric and imperial measurements, so no matter your country, you can enjoy these dishes. **Bon appétit!** (That one's French.)

A WORD ON PUNCTUATION

We're book people, so of course we love proper punctuation and spelling. Throughout this book, however, you will also see some *Neopets* item descriptions missing an apostrophe or perhaps having an incorrect ellipse. This is because *Neopets* sometimes goes by the British spelling, as noted above, and also because the system can't recognize apostrophes in item descriptions. So, what we're saying is: please don't write any angry "Letters to the Editor" about this! We just want to make this cookbook authentic and Neopian. You may, however, direct angry "Letters to the Editor" at anyone who spells **"Borovan"** incorrectly.

DON'T FORGET TO FEED YOUR

neopets®

Is your Neopet dying of hunger? Belly bloated with too many omelettes? Or are they checked happily into the Neolodge, where they're getting fed and pampered? No matter your Neopet's status (although you really should feed them), it's time to see if you have the cooking chops of Chef Bonju in the first-ever **The Official *Neopets* Cookbook!** (We know—we're excited too.)

Neopia is a dazzling land where the Neopets, Petpets, Petpetpets, and Faeries live. In this book, you'll feast on decadent Faerieland fare (like the Fyora Spring Soup, page 42) and Gnorbu Wool Noodles (page 56) from gorgeous Shenkuu, and you'll taste Illusen Biscotti (page 112) from none other than Meridell, just to name a few.

Of course, no trip to Neopia is complete without visiting Tyrannia's Giant Omelette or Jellyworld's Giant Jelly. Do not fret—recipes for omelettes and jellies are included in this book, as well as delightful Mynci Cristo Sandwiches (page 26), Pyramibread (and Toasted Pyramibread, if you prefer) (page 70), Checkerboard Pizza (page 30), Iced Fish Cake (page 84), and a whole lot more.

You'll get to relive the magic of Neopia in this gorgeous and eye-catching cookbook, with food fit for everyone, from picky eaters like that pesky

Christmas Kougra who won't eat pastries ("Yuck! I'm not eating one of those!") all the way to a very hungry Skeith who will eat that expensive Paint Brush if you leave it in your inventory too long.

Since we know that no two Neopets or Neopians are alike, the recipes enclosed in this book are made to be flexible. For example, if you prefer vegan options, you might substitute your favorite plant-based cheese or pressed tofu for the halloumi cheese in the Wocky Tacos (page 24), or if you prefer another flavor of Cantaloupe Slushie (page 110), you can always try cramming in a cheeseburger instead.

What's more, each recipe comes from Neopia itself, meaning that you can purchase each food with Neopoints and feed it to your pet (or in *one* case, rather than feed, customize it for your pet to wear with Neocash). Perhaps have a candlelit dinner for two—Neopian to Neopian—or invite a crew over for a Meridellian Feast. (Feasts always pair well with some late-night Destruct-O-Match III.)

No matter whether you're an active player, a returning Neopian, or simply love good food, we welcome you into the fold of Neopian cooking. And from all of us at Team *Neopets* Cookbook (which we've dubbed our staff of twenty-plus-year players), let's get cooking.

AND NOW, A MESSAGE FROM
The Soup Faerie

In the **Neopian marketplace**, there is a very large cauldron of soup. Here, less fortunate Neopians can visit the **Soup Kitchen** and feed their **Neopets** for free.

Some of the soups we serve at the Soup Kitchen include Cornupepper, asparagus and chutney, chicken and vegetable, and Negg Soup. What's important about the Soup Kitchen is that it seeks to help others–without asking anything in return.

If you choose to share any of these foods with family, friends, strangers, or even **Jhudora** and **Illusen**-like rivals, you invite a little bit of this kindness into your life. It would warm my heart to see Neopians visiting their own soup kitchens and stocking them with items or treats. Lately, I've been hearing of community fridges, which are fantastic options for donating food too.

In **Neopia**, there's also the **Money Tree**, where kind Neopians donate their unwanted items. Should you be so kind, please look into donating food or other items to those in your own communities.

Throughout this book, you'll get some **kind tips** from me on how to make foods allergy-friendly so that all guests can enjoy. But my biggest tip is to **always take care of those less fortunate**. You never know when that could be you!

Something has happened!

The Soup Faerie has invited the other Faeries to make comments throughout this book. You'll get helpful, kind tips and tricks from the Soup Faerie, regal plating tips from **QUEEN FYORA** of Faerieland, and maybe even a chaotic note or two from **JHUDORA** the Dark Faerie.

In *Neopets*, the Faeries give random quests during which users must find an item for the Faeries and get rewarded in return. This is much like cooking—find food, make food, and be rewarded when you eat!

ALL ABOUT NEOPIAN FOOD

food shop

There are hundreds of thousands of Neopian foods out there, so choosing just over 40 of them for this cookbook was quite a daunting task. In Neopia, there's even the **Gourmet Club**, which is an exclusive organization that **Neopets** can belong to if they've eaten tons of gourmet food. At the time of writing this, there are **1,418 foods** that qualify for a pet's entry in the Gourmet Club—and some of them, like the **Space Quesadilla (page 54)**, are included in this book.

Neopians can visit a variety of food places in **Neopia** as well, where they can purchase and feed their **Neopet** interesting foods. Some of those vendors include **Hubert's Hot Dogs**, the **Chocolate Factory**, **Pizzaroo**, the **Smoothie Store**, **Cafe Kreludor**, and **Qasalan Delights**. The recipes you'll find in this book range from **Poogle Sushi** (page 38) to **White Chocolate Grarrl Teeth** (page 98), and all are featured on the website.

KITCHEN SAFETY

Even in Neopia, pets can get hurt, which is why many Neopians bring their loved ones to **Faerieland's Healing Springs**, where the Water Faerie, **Marina**, bestows her healing magic. Unfortunately, no such magical Healing Springs exist outside of Neopia, so you must be very careful in the kitchen, where **Marina's** magic can't help you.

1 Before selecting your recipe, WASH YOUR HANDS WITH SOAP AND WATER. (Extra credit if you happen to have some Darigan Foamy Soap at your disposal.) Also make sure your kitchen surface is clean.

2 Even the Soup Faerie WEARS AN APRON—so don't forget one! This keeps your clothes clean. Tie back any loose hair too.

3 Ensure all fresh FOOD IS WASHED PROPERLY—you don't want any gross food, like a Rotten Negg and Onion Quesadilla, on your hands!

4 If cooking with young ones, make sure they are always supervised. These recipes are very fun to tackle as a team, but KEEP THE KNIVES FOR THE ADULTS, please. And put the Borovan down.

BOROVAN

You might be wondering . . . will this cookbook have a recipe for **Borovan**?

This is *Neopets: The Official Cookbook*. Of course it has Borovan. What do you think we are, newbies?!

Borovan is a hot drink served in Neopia, and you can make it at the Cooking Pot in Mystery Island by combining Hot Chocolate and Asparagus–yum! There are even cookbooks in Neopia all about Borovan, including *365.25 Borovan Recipes, Best Borovan Recipes,* and a delightful scratch-and-sniff, *Borovan: The Truth Behind the Smell.**

BOROVAN IS MY FAVOURITE!

DID YOU KNOW?

Adam, the creator of *Neopets*, uses the username borovan.

*Note: While these are books in Neopia that you can read to your pet, they are not, in fact, corporeal cookbooks. Unless you buy a ton of *Neopets: The Official Cookbook* copies and tell your friends and we get greenlit for a sequel. *365.25 Borovan Recipes*, here we come!

CUP OF HOT BOROVAN

Prep time: 5 minutes • Cooking time: 8 minutes • Makes 1 serving

This special recipe wasn't created for the cookbook; it's from **TNT**, aka The Official **Neopets** Team itself. To have the true Neopian experience, you may want to sip on some **Borovan** creations on a nice day.

"A lovely cup of hot Borovan. Borovan is good for you, it puts hairs on your chest!"

INGREDIENTS

6 spears raw asparagus

2 cups (16 fl. oz./475ml) water

1 tablespoon honey

1 cup (8 fl. oz./250ml) milk

½ cup (4 oz./115g) grated semisweet chocolate

½ teaspoon ground cinnamon

 **KIND TIP!**

To make this recipe vegan, simply swap the milk for plant-based milk and the honey for maple syrup. Many semisweet chocolates are dairy-free, but always check your labels to be sure. You can also use dark chocolate if preferred.

1. Wash and cut 5 raw asparagus spears into 2-inch pieces. Place the water in a small pan and add the cut asparagus. Heat on medium temperature and bring to a boil. Add the honey and let simmer for 5 minutes.

2. In a separate pan, heat up the milk on low heat and add the chocolate. Stir until melted and well blended. Add the cinnamon. Turn off the burner as steam starts to rise.

3. Remove the asparagus from the heat. Drain the asparagus and set aside for dinner later. Add the asparagus-and-honey-water blend to the milk-and-chocolate blend. Stir a few times and pour the mixture into a cup. Garnish with the remaining asparagus spear. Serve and enjoy!

I love Borovan because it uses some of Meridell's finest crops—asparagus spears.

SAVORY

COSMIC STARS SANDWICH

Prep time: 40 minutes, plus proofing • Cooking time: 40 minutes • Makes 4 sandwiches

This recipe is taken right from **Gargarox's** *Grundo Cafe Recipes*–and if you prefer enjoying the **Cosmic Cheese Stars** as a simple snack, they taste delicious without the bread too. Plus, the cheese stars are gluten-free. Mmm!

"How can you make cheese stars better? Put them in a sandwich of course!"

INGREDIENTS

FOR THE BREAD:

¼-ounce (7-g) packet dried yeast

1 teaspoon sugar

1½ cups (350ml) lukewarm water

3¾ cups (500g) bread flour, plus extra for dusting

1 teaspoon fine salt

Blue food coloring

Black food coloring

Oil, for greasing

FOR THE SANDWICH:

8 slices of your lovely blue bread

Slices of your favorite cheese, or a mixture of cheeses

Butter, for spreading

KIND TIP!

You can make these vegan by ensuring the cheese and butter are plant-based.

As a gluten-free option, make the cheese stars only for a simple yet satisfying snack.

1. Place the yeast and sugar in a pitcher and pour in the warm water. Make sure it's only lukewarm or it will kill the yeast. Stir until dissolved, then leave for a few minutes until it starts to look frothy on top.

2. Meanwhile, place the flour and salt in the bowl of a stand mixer fitted with a dough hook attachment. Pour the yeast mixture in and mix together roughly with a spoon. Add enough blue and black food coloring to create a deep-blue color, then knead with the machine for 8–10 minutes, until smooth and elastic. Grease a clean bowl with a little oil and transfer the dough to it, turning the dough over to coat it in the oil. Cover with a damp dish towel or plastic wrap and leave someplace warm to rise for about 1 hour, or until it has doubled in size.

3. Grease a 2-pound loaf pan with a little oil. Dust a clean surface lightly with flour and tip the dough out onto it. Knead briefly, then shape it into a rough oval. Fold the longer ends in, then fold in the sides to make a rough rectangle. Turn it over so the fold lines are underneath and place it into the prepared pan. Cover loosely and let rise for another 30 minutes. Meanwhile, preheat the oven to 220°F (105°C) and place an empty roasting pan on the bottom rack.

4. Once the dough has risen, remove the cover and place the pan in the oven. Pour ½ cup of water into the roasting pan—this will create steam and help give the bread a lovely crusty top. Bake for 20 minutes, then lower the heat to 375°F (190°C) and bake for a further 15–20 minutes. Remove from the pan and let cool on a wire rack until it reaches room temperature.

5. To make your sandwiches, remove the crusts from the slices of bread, as these will be a little brown and not super-space blue. Using star cookie cutters of various sizes, cut out cheese stars to stuff your sandwiches. Make sure you cut 4 smaller but quite thick cheese stars for decorating the tops.

6. Butter the bread. Lay out a piece of bread and add stars. Then affix another slice of bread on top. Spear your smaller stars with toothpicks (cocktail sticks) and insert through the middle of each sandwich to serve.

HOOOOME!

Something has happened!

A passing **BLUMAROO** hops over and says, "Did you know? Grundos are a Neopet that came to Neopia from their home on Kreludor. They inhabit the Space Station on Neopia, but the cheese stars remind them of home."

HOT DOG BURRITO

Prep time: 5 minutes • Cooking time: 15 minutes • Makes 4 burritos

You don't have to be a Hot Dog Hero to enjoy this **Hot Dog Burrito**, teeming with tasty onions and grated cheese. This delicacy can be purchased at **Hubert's Hot Dogs** or made in the comfort of your own kitchen. Just enjoy it while it's hot!

"The two champions of junk food finally meet in one delicious meal."

INGREDIENTS

Drizzle of oil

2 onions, finely sliced

2 teaspoons fajita seasoning (or more if you want it really spicy)

Pinch of salt

4 frankfurter hot dogs

4 tortillas

2 ounces (60g) grated cheese

Ketchup and yellow mustard, to taste

1. Heat the oil in a nonstick frying pan over medium heat and add the onion, fajita seasoning, and the pinch of salt. Fry for 10 minutes, stirring frequently, until the onions are really soft and well caramelized.

2. Meanwhile, cook the hot dogs in a pan of simmering water for a few minutes until piping hot throughout.

3. Lay the tortillas out on a work surface and divide the spicy onions among them, spreading them out in a line down the middle. Sprinkle cheese over the onions.

4. Add a hot dog to each burrito and finish with a drizzle of ketchup and/or mustard. Roll up and enjoy!

KIND TIP!

 For a vegan version, substitute with your favourite veggie hot dogs and plant-based cheese.

 For a gluten-free option, make sure your tortilla is gluten-free. I recommend corn or cassava tortillas.

Something has happened!

A **MAGMA USUL** says, "If you want your hot dogs to look extra fiery, instead of simmering them, you can cook them on a griddle pan until char lines appear on the outsides and they are piping hot throughout."

WOCKY TACOS

Prep time: 20 minutes • **Cooking time:** 10 minutes • **Makes 4 to 6 servings**

For a scrumptious delight, look no further than these **tacos**. The tortillas in this recipe are made to look like **Wocky faces**. Play around with the red cabbage to make your **Wocky Tacos**, er, hairy.

"The perfect blend of fur and cheese!"

INGREDIENTS

FOR THE PINK SLAW:

¼ small red cabbage, shredded

½ small red onion, finely sliced

1 small carrot, peeled and grated

½ cup (120g) mayonnaise (use vegan or low-fat, if preferred)

Salt and pepper

FOR THE TACOS:

2 8-ounce (225g) blocks halloumi cheese, each cut into 6 slices

1 tablespoon taco seasoning

12 small corn tortillas (ones that are slightly oval shaped are best)

Drizzle of oil

1. First, make the slaw. Combine all the ingredients in a large mixing bowl and stir together well. Season to taste with salt and pepper.

2. Pat the halloumi slices dry with paper towels, then lay them in a shallow dish and sprinkle half of the taco seasoning over them. Turn them over and sprinkle the other sides with the remaining seasoning.

3. Cut a rough rectangular-shaped wedge—with the two shorter ends curved—out of each side of the tortillas to make Wocky ears that will roughly line up when the tortilla is folded in half.

4. Heat a large nonstick frying pan over high heat. Place a tortilla in the pan and cook for a couple of minutes on each side until softened, darkening in spots and smelling toasty. Remove from the pan and fold loosely in half before it has time to cool and set flat. Repeat to shape and cook the rest of the tortillas.

4. Heat a drizzle of oil in a ridged griddle pan (or use the frying pan you cooked the tortillas in) over high heat and lay the halloumi slices in it. (You may have to do this in two batches.) Cook for a few minutes until there are lovely char lines appearing on the undersides of the slices, then flip over to cook the other sides.

5. Place a slice of halloumi into each taco, pile in the pink slaw, and serve immediately.

KIND TIP!

Make this vegan by using a plant-based mayo in the slaw and subbing pressed tofu or plant-based Mediterranean grill cheese for the halloumi.

MYNCI CRISTO SANDWICH

Prep time: 5 minutes • Cooking time: 8 minutes • Makes 1 sandwich

You don't have to be a **Mynci** to enjoy this scrumptious **Mynci Cristo Sandwich**. This sandwich is best enjoyed in the tropical forest of **Mystery Island**, although we suppose your dining table will do.

"Ham, Turkey, and Swiss Cheese all layered between two slices of bread. The sandwich is then fried and topped with powdered sugar and served with jam."

INGREDIENTS

Butter, for spreading

2 slices white bread

2 slices ham

2 slices turkey

2 slices Swiss cheese

Confectioners' sugar, for dusting

Raspberry jam, to serve

KIND TIP!

For a gluten-free version, simply use your favourite gluten-free bread.

1. Butter your slices of bread, then turn one over so it is butter side down on a cutting board. Add two slices each of ham, turkey, and Swiss cheese, and place the other slice on top, butter side up.

2. Heat a large nonstick frying pan over medium-low heat and add the sandwich to the pan. Cook for a few minutes until it starts to brown on the base, then flip it over and cook for a few minutes on the other side, until well browned and the cheese is melted.

3. Place a little confectioners' sugar in a small sieve and dust it over the top of the sandwich. Flip it over and cook for a few seconds until the sugar caramelizes. While that is cooking, dust what is now the top, then flip over to caramelize that side too.

4. Slice the sandwich in half diagonally, then serve with a side of raspberry jam.

Something has happened!

An **ORANGE MYNCI** says, "Although you can eat this Mynci Cristo Sandwich any day of the year, it is particularly delicious on Mynci Day, which takes places on the 22nd of the month of Awakening, aka February 22 every year."

CHEESY ASPARAGUS

Prep time: 15 minutes • Cooking time: 10 minutes • Makes 2 to 4 servings

Asparagus is a very popular food in **Neopia**. Asparagus is featured prominently in the Neopets Trading Card Game, it's a color that you can morph your **Chia** into, and it is even furniture that you can use to decorate your **Neohome** with. Not to mention, we think this dish pairs well with a nice **Cup of Hot Borovan**.

"All the green goodness of asparagus, smothered in finest cheddar cheese."

INGREDIENTS

FOR THE ASPARAGUS:

8 large asparagus spears

FOR THE CHEESE SAUCE:

2 tablespoons (1 oz./30g) butter

1 tablespoon cornstarch

1 cup (8 fl. oz./250ml) whole milk

½ cup (4¼ oz./120g) grated cheddar cheese

½ to 1 teaspoon Dijon mustard

Salt and freshly ground black pepper

1. Wash the asparagus, then snap or cut any woody ends off the asparagus spears. Bring a large pot of salted water to a boil.

2. While you are waiting for the water to boil, make the cheese sauce. Melt the butter in a saucepan, then stir in the cornstarch, whisking to make sure there are no lumps. Add the milk and cook for a few minutes, stirring frequently, until the sauce begins to thicken.

3. Stir in the cheese and mustard and continue to cook until the cheese is melted and the sauce is smooth. Season to taste with salt and pepper.

4. Once the water is boiling, drop in the asparagus spears and cook for just 3 to 4 minutes, or until the spears are tender but still very green with a bit of crunch. Drain them in a colander, then transfer to plates and top with the cheese sauce to serve.

Something has happened!

An **ASPARAGUS CHIA** says, "Asparagus is used to measure the Neopian economy. One bundle of asparagus should cost 9,763,815 NP per kilogram (which is 9,763,815,000 NP per gram!)"

KIND TIP!

If you'd like to make an alternate version, try **Asparagus and Hollandaise Sauce!** Swap the cheese sauce for your favourite Hollandaise and give it a go.

29

CHECKERBOARD PIZZA

Prep time: 30 minutes, plus proofing • Cooking time: 40 minutes • Makes 4 servings

For all the fun of checkers with all the taste of pizza, enjoy this Neopian **Checkerboard Pizza**. You'll need to arrange the checkers yourself, but by using olives and pepperoni, you can actually play the game! If it lasts that long—you might just want to scoop up a hot slice!

"Mmmmm... queen my pepperoni!"

INGREDIENTS

FOR THE CRUST:

¼-ounce (7-g) packet dried yeast

½ teaspoon granulated sugar

½ cup (4 fl. oz./125ml) warm water

1⅔ cups (9¼ oz./260g) white bread flour, plus extra for dusting

½ teaspoon salt

1 tablespoon olive oil, plus extra for greasing

FOR THE PIZZA SAUCE:

1¾ cups (14 oz./400g) tomato puree or passata

1 garlic clove, minced

½ teaspoon dried oregano

2 tablespoons olive oil

Sea salt and freshly ground black pepper

FOR THE TOPPINGS:

14 ounces (400g) mozzarella (block preferred, but you can also use shredded)

Large black olives

Small pepperoni slices

1. Place the yeast and sugar in a small bowl and pour in the water. Stir together, then set aside for a few minutes for the yeast to wake up.

2. Meanwhile, sift the flour and salt into a large mixing bowl and make a well in the center. Pour the yeast mixture and the olive oil into the well and use a dinner knife to mix it all together roughly.

3. Now get your hands in and begin to knead the dough, bringing it all together at first, then tipping it out onto a work surface to continue kneading for about 10 minutes, or until the dough is smooth and stretchy. (You can also do this in a stand mixer fitted with a dough hook.) Grease a bowl with a little olive oil and place the dough into it. Cover and leave in a warm place for 45 minutes to 1 hour, until the dough ball has doubled in size.

4. Once the dough has had its first rise, tip it onto a work surface, punch the air out, and divide it into 4 even pieces. Try to shape them into rough squares as you divide them—this will make it easier to roll them out to squares later. Place them on a baking sheet, cover again, and let them rise for another 30 minutes or so until almost doubled in size again.

5. Meanwhile, preheat your oven to its highest setting and place a pizza stone or heavy baking sheet in there to heat up.

6. Combine all the ingredients for the pizza sauce and season well with sea salt and pepper.

7. Dust a work surface very generously with flour. Take a portion of dough and roll it out thinly into a square. Keep moving the dough to make sure it hasn't stuck. Tidy up the edges by folding them over on all four sides to create a slightly raised wall around the outside of your square. Move the dough onto a well-floured baking sheet or a pizza peel if you have one. (A cake mover is also useful for this!)

THIS IS MY FAVOURITE FOOD!

8. Spread a quarter of the pizza sauce over the dough. Place squares of cheese in alternate rows (if using a block, which is preferred, cut into slices; if using shredded, arrange into squares) to look like a checkerboard. Top with olives and pepperoni to look like the checker pieces.

9. Open the oven door and quickly slide the pizza onto the hot pizza stone or baking sheet. Cook for about 10 minutes, or until the crust is cooked and the cheese melted and browning. Serve immediately and enjoy hot while you cook the other pizzas.

KIND TIP!

For a vegetarian version, swap the pepperoni for a plant-based version. For a vegan Checkerboard Pizza, also swap the cheese (if you want it nice and melty, brush some olive oil on top, and in the last two minutes of baking, switch to broil). To make this gluten-free, use a gluten-free baking flour at a 1:1 ratio.

BAKED FAERIE CORN

Prep time: 10 minutes • Cooking time: 20 minutes • Makes 4 servings

Faerie food is just different—it's regal, rich, and very buttery. This corn can be eaten as a side dish or a nice appetizer for a meal. It's favored by all the **Neopian Faeries**, and now you know why.

"Possibly the most delicious baked corn you will ever taste."

INGREDIENTS

FOR THE CORN:

4 ears corn, still in the husk

1 tablespoon olive oil

4 large pats salted butter

FOR THE "FAERIE DUST" (SEASONING):

1 teaspoon granulated garlic

1 teaspoon dried thyme

2 teaspoons flaky sea salt

½ teaspoon cayenne pepper

¼ teaspoon freshly ground black pepper

1. Preheat the oven to 350°F (180°C).

2. Remove the husks from the ears of corn and reserve them for later. Place the cobs on a large baking sheet and drizzle the olive oil over them. Using tongs, turn the corn cobs in the oil so that they are fully coated.

3. In a small bowl, combine all the ingredients for the faerie dust. Sprinkle it over the corn, again turning the corn so all the cobs are fully and evenly coated. Place the tray in the oven and bake for 15 to 20 minutes, until the corn is tender.

4. While the corn is baking, make the wings (see template on page 118). Using a pair of sharp kitchen scissors, cut wing shapes out of the corn husks. You will need one pair of large wings and one pair of tiny ones for each corn cob.

5. Once the corn is cooked, arrange the wing shapes on a serving plate in the shape of four butterflies with all the wings meeting in the middle. Place the ears of corn in the middle of the wings. Add a dollop of butter to each ear of corn and let it melt.

KIND TIP!

To make this recipe vegan, simply swap the butter for your favourite plant-based version.

I REALLY LIKE CORN.

HAUNTED HUMMUS

Prep time: 15 minutes • Makes 4 to 6 servings

Some Neopians say that **Haunted Hummus** is best served on Halloween, but we think it's a Spooky Food perfect for any day. We also love that this is vegan, vegetarian, and gluten-free optional.

"They say when the moon is full, this ghostly hummus will haunt the deserted pita..."

INGREDIENTS

1 14-ounce (400-g) can chickpeas

1 clove garlic, roughly chopped

2 tablespoons tahini

3 tablespoons extra-virgin olive oil

2 tablespoons fresh lemon juice

1 teaspoon ground cumin

Salt

2 large carrots

2 pita breads, warmed if wished

KIND TIP!

Simply omit the pita for a gluten-free version.

1. Start by draining the chickpeas, but reserve the water from the can. Place them into the food processor and add the garlic, tahini, olive oil, and lemon juice. Blend for 1 minute, stopping and scraping down the sides with a spatula occasionally so it's all blended to a smooth paste. This will take longer than you think, but persevere. Once you have a thick paste, add some of the aquafaba (the water from the chickpea can) to loosen it a little, but don't add too much—you need to be able to sculpt this into your ghoul! Taste, and season with the cumin and salt and blend again briefly.

2. To make your dippers, peel the carrots and chop into sticks. Pile these onto a serving dish and pop the pitas on top.

3. Spoon the hummus onto the bread, shaping it into a high mound as you go. Use a knife, your fingers, or whatever you find it easiest to mold with to create eyes and a mouth in your hummus mound. The mouth is easiest to make by using a (clean!) finger to scrape out a row of short vertical lines. For the eyes, try finding a wide knife (such as a palette knife) and inserting it into the hummus slightly on the diagonal. Then turn the outer side of the knife, keeping the other side in place at the inner corner of the eye, to create a fan shape in the hummus.

Something has happened!

A **GHOST MEERCA** appears in front of you! But it's friendly, not scary. The Ghost Meerca says, "If you prefer pita chips to pita bread, arrange them in a blue bowl for the classic Neopian food **Bowl of Pita Chips!**"

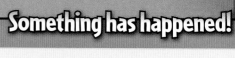

MERIDELLIAN-STYLE MASHED POTATOES

Prep time: 10 minutes • Cooking time: 20 minutes • Makes 4 servings

Meridell is a **Neopian** medieval land. It is home to **Ixis and Draiks**, as well as **Meridell Castle** and the **Darigan Citadel**. For a traditional Meridellian meal, enjoy these **Meridellian-Style Mashed Potatoes** with sausages, gravy, and cabbage. But whatever you do, you can't forget the flag.

"What a cute little flag!"

INGREDIENTS

2 pounds 4 ounces (1kg) potatoes, peeled and chopped into large chunks

3½ tablespoons (1¾ oz./50g) salted butter

2 tablespoons milk, plus extra if needed

3½ ounces (100g) grated Swiss cheese

Salt and freshly ground black pepper

Sausages, cabbage, and gravy, to serve

1. Place your potatoes in a large pot of salted water and bring it to a boil. Cook for about 20 minutes, depending on the size of your chunks, or until the potatoes are completely tender.

2. Drain the potatoes in a colander over the sink and leave them to steam-dry for a couple of minutes. Tip them back into the hot pan and add the butter, milk, and cheese. With a potato masher or ricer, mash the potatoes until smooth. Add a splash more milk if you need to.

3. Taste, and season with salt and pepper, then serve them piled into a mountain with a Meridellian flag (see template on page 121) on top to stake your claim, alongside sausages and cabbage and all swimming in gravy.

Something has happened!

A **ROYAL EYRIE** says, "Meridell is home to Darigan Citadel, which is ruled by Lord Darigan. Although originally seen as a villain, Lord Darigan helped defend Lord Kass, who threatened to overtake all of Meridell. Thankfully, all Meridellians can enjoy these potatoes, Darigan or not."

KIND TIP!

🌿 Swap the sausage for a plant-based version and treat yourself to a vegetarian meal!

🌷 This dish also tastes nice with plant-based milk, cheese, and butter, if preferred.

POOGLE SUSHI

Prep time: 30 minutes • Cooking time: 25 minutes • Makes 18 pieces

Poogles are cute, friendly looking Neopets—but don't be fooled! They have razor-sharp teeth. Originating from **Faerieland**, these Neopets are also the star of **Poogle Racing**. Of course, amateur sushi rollers might want to sharpen their skills at Culinary Concoctions in **Shenkuu**, where you may select any three Neopian foods in your inventory and see what happens.

"Sushi in the shape of a Poogle... how clever!"

INGREDIENTS

FOR THE SUSHI:

7 ounces (200g) raw sushi-grade tuna, in one large piece

1 ripe mango

3 sheets sushi nori

3 teaspoons gluten-free wasabi paste, or to taste

3 tablespoons toasted sesame seeds

FOR THE RICE:

Scant 1½ cups (9 oz./250g) sushi rice

3 tablespoons rice vinegar

1 teaspoon granulated sugar

1 teaspoon salt

KIND TIP!

For a vegan or vegetarian version, use a plant-based fish. If you prefer, you can use avocado, although your Poogles will look a little snotty.

1. First, cook the rice. Place it in a saucepan and add 1½ cups (375ml) water. Cover and cook for 10 minutes, then turn the heat off (don't remove the lid!) and let it steam for another 15 minutes.

2. Meanwhile, divide the tuna into three large, chunky strips the width of the nori sheet—you can piece two or three strips together if they aren't long enough.

3. Slice a cheek off the mango, cutting down one side of the stone. Slice that piece widthwise into ⅙-inch-thick (4- to 5-mm) strips. Take a strip of mango and cut off the skin, curving the knife as you do to create a more rounded semicircle (see photo opposite). Chop each pointed end off your slice. As you cut, carefully position your knife so that you curve the mango to fit snugly around your roll. Set the two ears to one side and repeat to make 18 sets of ears in total. If you run out of slices that are big enough to cut the ears from, simply slice the cheek off the other half of the mango and use that.

4. Once the rice has cooked, add the vinegar, sugar, and salt, and stir. Lay out a sheet of nori on a sushi rolling mat. Wet your hand and spread a third of the rice over the nori sheet, leaving a bare space along the far edge for sealing. Spread a teaspoon of the wasabi paste in a line on top of the rice, followed by a line of the toasted sesame seeds. Lay a strip of tuna on top. Starting from the side closest to you, use the mat to help you roll the rice up and over the tuna strip and then around into a roll. When the roll is almost fully rolled and you are up to the bare strip, lift the mat out of the way and finish rolling up the sheet. Place the roll, seam side down, to the side for a few minutes and the moisture from the rice will soak through the paper and seal it. Meanwhile, roll up the other sheets in the same way. Cut each long roll evenly into 6 pieces.

5. To finish your Poogle-shaped sushi, carefully insert a toothpick through each of the rolls, positioning it just above center. Insert one of your mango Poogle ears onto each end of the protruding stick, so that they stick out from the roll. Enjoy!

I recommend pairing with tamari sauce to serve.

KIND TIP!

Shaping the mango Poogle ears is simple—just follow the instructions opposite and use this picture for reference.

PIRATE SHIP DEVILED EGGS

Prep time: 30 minutes • Cooking time: 8 minutes • Makes 8 ships

These **Pirate Ship Deviled Eggs** are made to look like the exact ships that pirates sailed to discover **Krawk Island**. On Krawk Island, **Neopians** can visit the **Dubloon-O-Matic**, **Warf Wharf**, or–if they are lucky enough to hold all pieces of the map–the **Forgotten Shore**. These eggs are delicious and can be served as an appetizer, party snack, or whatever strikes your fancy.

"Pepper the sails with cannon fire, lads! Prove yer worth yer salt!"

INGREDIENTS

6 large eggs

3 tablespoons mayonnaise

½ teaspoon English or Dijon mustard (depending how hot you want them)

Pinch of smoked paprika

Pinch of salt

1. Boil a large pot of water and gently lower the eggs in. Cook for 7 to 8 minutes until hard boiled. Be careful not to overcook the eggs or they will start to turn grey. (The Grey Faerie likely has something to do with it!) Place the pot under cold running water and leave for a few minutes until the eggs cool down and stop cooking.

2. Once cool, peel the eggs and slice each one in half lengthwise. Carefully extract the yolks from them all and place them in a bowl. Then select the best 8 egg white halves to use as boats and set them aside. (The remaining four halves can be eaten straight away or stirred into mayo for a nice egg sandwich.)

3. In the bowl with the egg yolks, add the mayonnaise, mustard, paprika, and salt. Give everything a good stir, mashing the yolks up as you go, until you have a smooth filling. Adjust to taste with more mustard, paprika, or salt until you have the flavor you want.

4. Now you can either spoon the filling back into the holes in your reserved egg white boats, or, if you're feeling fancy, you can spoon it into a piping bag fitted with a large star tip and pipe it back in.

5. Finish each boat with a skull-and-crossbones flag, pop them on a serving platter (that's preferably as blue as the sea), and set them a-sail on your buffet table.

To make the flags, photocopy the flag template on page 121 eight times, then cut them out. Use a skewer to make two holes in the centre of the flag—one above and one below the skull—then insert a short wooden skewer into each one, as pictured.

FYORA SPRING SOUP

Prep time: 15 minutes • Cooking time: 30 minutes • Makes 4 servings

Legend has it this is **Queen Fyora's** favorite soup, made from some of the finest Faerie elements. Although it may seem odd, nasturtiums have a lovely peppery tingle similar to arugula. This nice, light soup has a pepper kick, perhaps from its Earth faerie origin.

"This delicious soup is made with edible flowers."

INGREDIENTS

- 1 tablespoon vegan butter
- 1 tablespoon extra-virgin olive oil
- ½ onion, finely diced
- 1 pound 5 ounces (600g) roughly chopped carrots
- 1 large stick celery, roughly chopped
- 1 clove garlic, finely chopped
- 3½ ounces (100g) nasturtium stems and flowers, stems roughly chopped, plus more flowers to serve
- 3½ cups (28 fl. oz./800ml) vegetable stock
- Sea salt and freshly ground black pepper

1. Melt the butter with the oil in a large saucepan over medium-low heat. Add the onion and cook for 5 minutes until beginning to soften. Add the carrots, celery, garlic, and any thick nasturtium stems and cook for 5 minutes.

2. Add the stock and cook for about 20 minutes, or until the carrots are tender. Add all the nasturtium stems and cook for about 2 minutes, just until the stems are wilted down.

3. Remove the pan from the heat and blend with an immersion blender until smooth. Taste, and season well with the sea salt and pepper.

4. Ladle into bowls and garnish each bowl with a couple of fresh flowers, to serve.

Something has happened

QUEEN FYORA floats by and says, "Nasturtiums can be found wherever plants are sold, but for those with a green thumb, you can easily care and tend to them too. Nasturtiums are incredibly vigorous and self-seed everywhere, so this is a great way to use them."

SKEITH BURGER

Everyone loves burgers, but perhaps no Neopet loves burgers more than **Skeiths**. Skeiths are scaly Neopets who are seen throughout Neopia. Most famous among them are the National Neopian Bank Manager, **King Hagan of Brightvale**; King Hagan's brother, **King Skarl of Meridell**; and **Snargan**, who oversees "Double or Nothing." All these Skeiths adore burgers, which you can enjoy whenever you please.

"OM NOM NOM..."

INGREDIENTS

4 ¼-pound hamburger patties

4 slices cheese

4 brioche burger buns, sliced in half

Mayonnaise, for spreading

Several small lettuce leaves

2 large tomatoes, sliced

Ketchup or relish (optional)

Tortilla chips

KIND TIP!

 Swap the beef patties for your favourite vegetarian version.

 Use a vegan patty, replace the cheese with plant-based cheese; the mayo with vegan mayo; and the brioche for hamburger buns without milk, honey, or egg.

 For a gluten-free version, use gluten-free buns and ensure the tortilla chips are derived only from gluten-free ingredients like cassava or corn.

1. Heat a ridged griddle pan over high heat—or fire up the outside grill. Place the hamburger patties on the griddle or grill and cook for a few minutes on each side, until well browned on the exterior and cooked to your liking in the center. Remove the patties from the griddle to a plate and place a cheese slice over each one. The cheese will begin to melt from the heat of the patties.

2. Place the burger bun halves, cut sides down, onto the griddle—you'll probably have to do these two at a time. Cook for a few seconds until char lines appear, then remove from the heat.

3. Spread a little mayo over the base of each bun and add a lettuce leaf to each. Add a couple of tomato slices, then place a hamburger patty with cheese on top of each one. Add ketchup or relish, if desired.

4. Snap the pointy corners off a few tortilla chips—you will need about 8 per burger. Using a small, sharp knife, cut slits in the tops of your burger buns and insert the tortilla corners to create Skeith spines.

5. Place the spiny bun tops on top of the burgers and serve!

I like eating it with Jhudora Fries, of course.

44

YURBLE POT PIE

Prep time: 30 minutes • Cooking time: 1¼ hours • Makes 4 to 6 servings

Cozy and inviting, this **Yurble Pot Pie** is a great dish to snuggle up with in winter—or to enjoy on a rainy summer's day. Yurbles are furry Neopets that are found all over Neopia, although perhaps most famous is the **Yurble Farmer**, who resides in **Meridell**.

"Made from fresh Yurb- just kidding!"

INGREDIENTS

FOR THE FILLING:

2 tablespoons olive oil

1 pound 12 ounces (800g) chicken thighs, chopped into large chunks

1½ tablespoons (1 oz./25g) butter

1 large onion, diced

1 pound 2 ounces (500g) sliced leeks

3 large cloves garlic, finely chopped

½ cup (4 fl. oz./125ml) white wine

1 cube chicken bouillon

2 teaspoons Dijon or whole-grain mustard

1 tablespoon cornstarch

½ cup (120g) full-fat crème fraîche

1 large handful fresh tarragon, leaves finely chopped

Sea salt and freshly ground black pepper

FOR THE PASTRY TOP:

1 pound 2 ounces (500g) puff pastry block

Flour, for dusting

1 egg, beaten

1. Start by making the pie filling. Heat the oil in a large nonstick sauté pan over high heat and add half the chicken. Cook for a few minutes, turning regularly, until browned all over. Remove from the pan with a slotted spoon, leaving the fat in the pan. Repeat to brown the second half of the chicken, removing that from the pan once done too.

2. Turn the heat under the pan down to medium-low and add the butter. Let it melt, then add the onion and cook for about 5 minutes, or until it begins softening. Add the leeks and garlic and cook for another 5 minutes or so, or until everything is tender. Return the browned chicken to the pan.

3. Add the white wine to the pan and cook for 2 to 3 minutes to reduce by half. Meanwhile, dissolve the bouillon cube in ½ cup (4 fl. oz./120ml) boiling water. Add this to the pan, too, along with the mustard. Mix the cornstarch with a splash of cold water to a smooth paste, then add this to the pan and cook for a few minutes until the sauce thickens. Turn off the heat and stir in the crème fraîche and tarragon. Season to taste with salt and pepper, then tip the contents of the pan into a pie dish and allow to cool.

Continues on next page!

Thanks, you are the best owner in the world!

4. Roll out three-quarters of the pastry on a lightly floured work surface to about ⅙ inch (4mm) thick and cut out a circle the size of your pie dish. Brush the lip of your dish with a little beaten egg and lay the pastry circle over the top. Crimp the edges to seal, then brush the whole top with beaten egg.

5. Photocopy and print out the template on page 119 at 200 percent of the size. Roll out the remaining pastry and place the template over it. Use a sharp knife to cut around it to make the shape of a Yurble. Use the template as a guide to score in the eyes and other details. Place your pastry Yurble on top of the pie; it will stick to the egg glaze. Glaze the top of the Yurble too. Place the pie in the fridge to chill while you preheat the oven to 350°F (180°C).

6. Bake the pie for about 45 minutes, until the filling is piping hot and the crust is risen and golden. Serve immediately, but make sure to cool off bites before eating.

KIND TIP!

To make the Yurble Pot Pie dairy-free, simply use a plant-based butter and a plant-based buttercream for the crème fraîche and ensure the puff pastry does not contain butter.

PTERI KABOB

Prep time: 10 minutes • Cooking time: 10 minutes • Makes 8 kabobs

Kabobs, anyone? Come get your **Pteri Kabobs**, fresh off the grill! Of course, this version doesn't have real **Pteris**–it's naturally vegetarian, with mushrooms representing the baby birds. **Pteris** are native to **Tyrannia**, where the kabobs can be eaten when left out in the hot sun.

"These are best after being cooked on the barbeque."

INGREDIENTS

- 16 small baby button mushrooms with plenty of stalk
- 16 cherry tomatoes
- 1 small zucchini, sliced
- ½ yellow bell pepper, diced to match size of mushrooms
- 7-ounce (200-g) block halloumi, sliced into cubes
- Olive oil, for brushing
- Spice mix of your choice, such as fajita, jerk, etc.

1. First, prepare your Pteri heads. Slice a mushroom stalk lengthwise along the stalk on a diagonal, so it's sharpened to a point. Shave off the bottom of the mushroom under the stalk to flatten the base, then use a skewer to poke an eye into the mushroom. Repeat to make 16 bird heads.

2. Thread your Pteri heads onto 8 skewers, alternating with the cherry tomatoes, zucchini slices, pepper slices, and halloumi chunks.

3. Brush your kabobs with a little oil using a pastry brush, then sprinkle over your seasoning mix.

4. Cook these on a barbeque for best results. Or if inside, heat a griddle pan over medium-high heat and add your kabobs—you may have to cook them in two batches, depending on the size of your pan. Cook for a few minutes on each side, until everything is cooked, then serve hot.

KIND TIP!

To make these vegan, use your favourite plant-based grill cheese or omit the halloumi entirely.

SQUAWK! HAHA, TRY POSTING THAT ON THE NEOBOARDS!

Something has happened!

If you have a **PTERI** and are visited by the **GOLDEN PTERI**, you may get special prizes, like Neopoints. Always best to have a Pteri!

NEGG LASAGNA

Prep time: 40 minutes • Cooking time: 1½ hours • Makes 6 servings

Neggs are Neopian food that are magical—some Neggs, like the **Power Negg**, give your Neopet an extra strength point, and some Neggs, like the **Plaid Egg**, may even change your Neopet's color. Since Neggs are so popular, there's even a **Negg Faerie** named **Kari** who oversees the **Neggery**, where Neggs are sold. This lasagna celebrates the best of Neggs and delicious, tomato-y pasta.

"This delicious lasagna is meat-free and made almost entirely out of neggs. This was given out as a prize for the Y15 Festival of Neggs."

INGREDIENTS

FOR THE RAGU:
2 tablespoons olive oil
1 large onion, finely diced
1 carrot, peeled and finely diced
1 large celery stalk, finely diced
1 red bell pepper, diced
1 large zucchini, finely diced
3 cloves garlic, finely chopped
14 ounces (400g) plant-based
　ground protein or meat
2 14-ounce (400g) cans
　chopped tomatoes
2 tablespoons tomato paste
3½ ounces (90g) dried Puy
　lentils
1 cube vegetable bouillon
Scant ½ cup (3½ fl. oz./100ml)
　red wine
Salt and black pepper

FOR THE BÉCHAMEL SAUCE:
8 tablespoons (4½ oz./120g)
　butter, plus extra for greasing
¾ cup (3½ oz./100g)
　all-purpose flour
4¼ cups (35 fl. oz./1L)
　whole milk

FOR THE LASAGNA:
10 to 12 sheets dried
　no-precook lasagna noodles
1/3 cup (1¾ oz./50g) grated
　cheddar cheese
5 large scallions

1. First, make the ragu. Heat the oil in a large saucepan and add the onion. Sauté gently for 5 minutes until the onion begins softening. Add the carrot, celery, bell pepper, and zucchini, and cook for another 5 minutes until they are beginning to soften too. Add the garlic, cook for 30 seconds or so, then add in the protein. Cook, stirring frequently, until the protein is browned, then add the tomatoes, tomato paste, and Puy lentils and stir.

2. Dissolve the bouillon cube in 2 cups (17 fl. oz./500ml) hot water and add to the pan, along with the red wine. Stir everything together, then leave to simmer, partly covering the pan, for 30 minutes, stirring occasionally. It should still be a little loose when cooked, as the pasta will absorb some of the water during cooking. If it has cooked down too much, just add a splash of water to loosen it a little.

3. Toward the end of the ragu's cooking time, prepare the béchamel sauce. Melt the butter in a large saucepan over low heat. Add the flour and whisk in, then let it cook for 2 to 3 minutes so that the taste of raw flour is cooked out. Add the milk a little at a time, whisking well between each addition, to form a smooth, lump-free sauce. As soon as the sauce is quite loose, you can add the rest of the milk at once. Continue to cook the sauce for about 5 minutes, until it starts to thicken. Once thick, but still pourable, remove it from the heat and season with salt. Preheat the oven to 350°F (180°C).

4. Once the ragu is cooked, season to taste with the salt and pepper. Grease a lasagna dish with the butter. Spread one-third of the ragu mixture over the base of the dish, then cover it completely with the dried lasagna noodles. Spread one-third of the béchamel sauce over the top of the pasta sheets.

5. Repeat the process, spreading another third of the ragu over the béchamel layer, then adding another layer of pasta and another layer of béchamel. Finally, do it one more time using the final third of the ragu, pasta, and béchamel, finishing with the béchamel on the top. Sprinkle the grated cheese over the top of the lasagna, and pop in the oven for about 45 minutes, or until the pasta is cooked and the top is browned and bubbling.

I LOVE NEGGS!

Aren't Neggs the best?

6. While the lasagna cooks, make your Negg stems. Trim the roots off the scallions—leaving a 2-inch (5-cm) length of stem intact at the root end of each—and trim away any tough green leaves. Place a scallion on a board and slice through the leaves lengthwise several times so that they are shredded like a tassel. Place the scallion in a bowl of cold water; the leaves will curl up. Repeat to make 5 more stems.

7. Once the lasagna is cooked, divide it into 6 portions, insert a scallion stem into the middle of each one, and serve!

KIND TIP!

To make this recipe gluten-free, swap for gluten-free lasagna sheets. Also swap the flour in the sauce for an alternative, such as arrowroot powder or cornstarch. Be sure your plant-based protein is gluten-free too.

To make it vegan, use vegan butter, milk, and cheese as well (I recommend cashew milk to mimic the béchamel's creaminess). Many dried lasagna noodles are already vegan, but always check your labels to be sure they don't contain egg.

53

SPACE QUESADILLA

Prep time: 20 minutes • Cooking time: 20 minutes • Makes 4 quesadillas

Ooey-gooey cheese meets space in this decadent dish that's sure to be a crowd-pleaser. Neopia's own **Space Faerie, Mira**, is rumored to love these quesadillas herself. You can use a cookie cutter for this recipe or create the shape on your own—both taste delicious!

"We used a cookie cutter to cut out star shapes as a reminder that this is no ordinary quesadilla."

INGREDIENTS

FOR THE QUESADILLAS:

1 tablespoon olive oil

1 small red onion, very finely diced

2 teaspoons ground cumin

1 teaspoon ancho chili flakes

2 cloves garlic, finely chopped

1 14-ounce (400-g) can pinto beans, drained

Squeeze of lime juice

Pinch of salt

8 tortillas (use corn if gluten-free)

11¼ ounces (320g) cheese— use a good melty one such as cheddar or Swiss, or a mixture of both

FOR THE PICO DE GALLO:

1 small red onion, finely diced

4 ripe tomatoes, deseeded and finely diced

1 large handful cilantro, finely chopped

Juice of 1 lime

2 tablespoons olive oil

Salt, for seasoning

1. To make the quesadilla filling, heat the oil in a saucepan over medium-low heat and add the onion. Cook for 5 minutes until well softened. Add the cumin, chili flakes, and garlic and cook for 2 to 3 minutes, then add the beans. Cook for 2 to 3 more minutes, then add in the lime juice and season with the salt. Mash the mixture with a potato masher until you have a chunky purée.

2. To make the pico de gallo, combine all the ingredients in a small bowl and season with salt, to taste.

3. Set a large nonstick frying pan over medium heat to warm up.

4. Lay out a tortilla and spread a quarter of the bean mixture over it using the back of a spoon or a stepped palette knife. Sprinkle over one-fourth of the cheese and place another tortilla on top. Press down to squish everything together. Use a large star-shaped cookie cutter to cut out as many stars as you can from the filled tortilla. Transfer the quesadillas to the hot pan and cook for about 3 minutes on each side until they are browning and crisp and the cheese is melting.

5. Serve the quesadillas immediately with the salsa spooned over the top and let people dig in while you cook the others in the same way—these are best fresh from the pan while the cheese is still molten! If you're still hungry, cook the star offcuts and eat those too!

Something has happened!

A passing **SPONGE AISHA** says, "Dr. Sloth, who tried to take over Neopia, was defeated by the Space Faerie and a Cybunny named Cylara. But nobody ever tried to get them in the same room and share Space Quesadillas . . . maybe it would have made a difference—who knows!"

This Space Quesadilla puts me in a good mood!

KIND TIP!

To make this dish vegan, swap for a plant-based cheese. Just make sure it's one that gets really melty. A tip for melty vegan cheese—brush some olive oil on it!

55

GNORBU WOOL NOODLES

Prep time: 20 minutes • **Cooking time: 30 minutes** • **Makes 4 servings**

Gnorbus are fun-loving and social Neopets. Famous Gnorbus include **Princess Terrana**, a member of **Shenkuu's royal family**, as well as **Professor Lambert**, who hails from **Brightvale**. These Shenkuu-inspired Gnorbu Wool Noodles are rumored to be loved by **Princess Terrana** herself. They are quite delicious with the right amount of heart.

"Noodles topped by wool balls and served in a Gnorbu shaped bowl."

INGREDIENTS

FOR THE SOUP:

2 cups (16 fl. oz./500ml) chicken stock

A few large slices ginger

1 clove garlic, sliced

6 fresh kaffir lime leaves

1 green chile, halved

12 ounces (350g) dried rice noodles

1 14-ounce (400-g) can coconut milk

Lime wedges, to serve

FOR THE DUMPLINGS:

16 to 20 or 14 ounces (400g) raw jumbo shrimp

1 tablespoon grated ginger

3 whole scallions

2 large egg whites

2 tablespoons cornstarch

1 teaspoon salt

1. Place the chicken stock in a saucepan and add the ginger, garlic, lime leaves, and chile. Leave it to simmer, covered, over medium-low heat for about 20 minutes, or until the stock is infused with all the flavors.

2. Meanwhile, make the dumplings. Place the shrimp, ginger, and scallions in a food processor and pulse a few times to blend the mixture to a chunky paste. Add the egg whites and blend them in, then add the cornstarch and salt, and pulse again until everything is well combined.

3. Get another saucepan of water boiling and cook the rice noodles according to the packet instructions.

4. Taste the stock and check it's well flavored (it will be watered down in a moment, so it needs to be quite strong), then strain it and return it to the saucepan. Add the coconut milk to the pan and stir in, then keep cooking over medium heat until it warms up again. Taste again and season to taste with salt.

5. Scoop balls of the shrimp mixture with your hands, each about the size of a walnut. You are aiming to get 12 balls in total. The mixture will be quite loose and sticky but will set as it cooks, so just scoop one at a time, dropping them into the hot soup as you go—raggedy and fluffy is good here, as these are your cotton wool. Cook gently for 4 to 5 minutes, until the dumplings are cooked through.

6. Once the noodles are cooked, drain them and add them to the soup pan, and turn everything to coat. Divide the noodles among four bowls and arrange the dumplings on top. Pour the remaining coconutty broth over the noodles in the bowls. Serve with lime wedges for squeezing.

MEATY ASPARAGUS DISH

Prep time: 5 minutes • Cooking time: 10 minutes • Makes 4 servings

For when you're craving asparagus but also want to enjoy a bit of meat too, look no further than this scrumptious meal. Feeling extra hungry? You can double the portion of meat for a **Meatier Asparagus Dish!**

"Tasty asparagus paired with a few pieces of meat."

INGREDIENTS

- 2 tablespoons olive oil, plus a drizzle for the steak
- 2 large echalion shallots, halved lengthways and finely sliced
- 2 garlic cloves, minced
- Leaves from a few sprigs of fresh thyme
- 14 ounces (400g) asparagus spears, chopped into 2-inch (5-cm) lengths
- 4 sirloin steaks, sliced into thick strips
- 2 teaspoons Worcestershire sauce
- Squeeze of lemon juice
- Salt and black pepper

KIND TIP!

You can make this recipe vegan by ensuring the meat is plant-based. I recommend soy curls or seitan for this recipe. Many Worcestershire sauces are already vegan, but check your label to be sure. One catch—you must call your creation the "**Unmeaty Asparagus Dish**," since . . . well, you know.

1. Heat the oil in a nonstick frying pan over medium heat and add the shallots. Sauté for a few minutes until they begin to soften. Add the garlic and thyme leaves and cook for another minute before adding the asparagus. Continue to sauté everything for another 3 to 4 minutes, or until the asparagus is tender but still has a little crunch. Transfer everything to a plate and cover with aluminum foil to keep warm.

2. Add another drizzle of oil to the pan and turn up the heat to high. Once very hot, add half the steak and sear over high heat for a minute or so until browned on the outside but still a little pink in the middle. Tip the first batch onto the plate with the vegetables, add another drizzle of oil to the pan, and sear the second batch in the same way.

3. Return the vegetables and first batch of steak to the pan and quickly stir in the Worcestershire sauce and the lemon juice. Season with the salt and pepper to taste, then divide among 4 plates and serve immediately.

OMELETTES

THE GIANT OMELETTE

One of the most popular places in all Neopia is the **Giant Omelette**. The Giant Omelette is in **Tyrannia**, and it is guarded by a Lupe named **Sabre-X**. Those who approach the Giant Omelette and manage to take a slice are rewarded quite handsomely—aka, with a slice of omelette.

Tyrannia is hot, meaning that its surface is the perfect temperature to cook an egg. Thus the **Giant Omelette** gets its power!

There are many omelettes that users can take from the **Giant Omelette**, and if we were to include them all, we'd have just a recipe book of omelettes (which doesn't sound so bad, but we're a little partial to Neopian sweets too!). As such, you'll get a recipe for a Plain Omelette, and you can add different toppings to make a variety of different omelettes, such as:

See photo of this on page 61!

- Bacon and Broccoli Omelette
- Bacon Omelette
- BBQ Sauce Omelette
- Black Currant Omelette
- Carrot and Pea Omelette
- Cheese and Onion Omelette
- Cheese Omelette
- Chocolate Omelette
- Chokato Omelette
  (if you can find Chokatos IRL, that is)
- Clay Omelette
  (maybe don't eat this one)
- Fresh Fruit Surprise Omelette
- Green Pepper Omelette
- Ham and Cheese Omelette
- Honey Blossom Omelette
- Hot Tyrannian Pepper Omelette
- Juppie Omelette
- Little Fishy Omelette

- Marshmallow Omelette
- Meat Feast Omelette
- Mushroom Omelette
- Pizza Omelette
- Rice Omelette
- Rotten Omelette
- Sausage and Pepperoni Omelette
- Sausage Omelette
- Spicy Red Pepper Omelette
- Spinach Feta Omelette
- Strawberry Omelette
- Tangy Tigersquash Omelette
- Tomato and Pepper Omelette
- Tomato Omelette
- Twirly Fruit Omelette
- Ugga Melon Omelette
- Veggie Delight Omelette

PLAIN OMELETTE

Prep time: 2 minutes • Cooking time: 3 minutes • Makes 1 omelette

A favorite **Tyrannian** food, this **Plain Omelette** is the base for many scrumptious breakfasts that you can eat in **Neopia**. Simply cook this in a skillet and season as desired.

"Just a plain omelette, yum yum that eggy flavour is just too much!"

INGREDIENTS

3 eggs
Sea salt and freshly ground
    black pepper
1 tablespoon butter

KIND TIP!

To make this dairy-free, use olive or avocado oil instead of butter, but reduce the heat to make sure it doesn't burn. Some liquid egg substitutes, like Just Egg, work well for a vegan version.

BONUS!

To get that Neopian omelette square shape, once folded, trim it square with a knife (and secretly eat the offcuts!).

1. Crack the eggs into a bowl. Season well with salt and pepper and beat them with a fork.

2. Heat a small, nonstick, heavy-based skillet over medium-high heat and add the butter. Once the pan is hot and the butter has melted, pour the egg mixture into the pan. Move it around the base a little, scraping it up with a fork and letting uncooked egg run into the holes and cook.

3. Once the bottom is set but it's still a little runny on top, shake the pan to shuffle the omelette so one edge comes up the side of the pan. Get a spatula and flip it over the top. Then shuffle it to the other edge of the pan, and flip the other side in so it's folded into thirds. If you are adding additional ingredients to your omelette, such as mushrooms, bacon, etc., sprinkle them down the middle before flipping the sides over them to cover. Make sure to get this as square as possible to resemble the Neopian omelettes.

4. Flip the omelette out onto a plate and serve immediately.

MUSHROOM OMELETTE

Prep time: 5 minutes • Cooking time: 10 minutes • Makes 1 omelette

Users can purchase an **Organic Mushroom** at the shop Neopian Health Foods–or you can find your favorite mushrooms at your local store or **farmer's market**.

"Eating this omelette requires a great love of mushrooms. Not only are they on top, but they are also inside AND mixed with the egg."

INGREDIENTS

2 ounces (60g) small mushrooms, such as white button or cremini

1 tablespoon butter or avocado oil

Plain Omelette (opposite page)

1. Slice the mushrooms. Heat the butter or avocado oil in a small skillet and fry the mushrooms until they are golden brown. Keep them warm until you are ready to add them to your omelette.

2. Make a Plain Omelette (see opposite), and when ready to add additional ingredients to the omelette, add in three-fourths of the mushrooms.

3. Flip the omelette out and top with the remaining mushrooms. You may use tongs to decorate—just be careful not to touch them, as they'll be hot!

MMM, MUSHROOM-Y!

BONUS!
If you want to taste the omelette before serving to a guest, simply take a big bite out of it. 2/3 Mushroom Omelette tastes just as delicious.

TOMATO AND PEPPER OMELETTE

Prep time: 5 minutes • Cooking time: 10 minutes • Makes 1 omelette

Juicy tomato and zesty pepper pair perfectly in this omelette, which will be sure to satisfy vegetarians and eaters of all kinds.

"Tomato and Pepper omelette is rarely found due to its unique flavour, but Im sure your Neopet is going to enjoy it."

INGREDIENTS

1 tablespoon olive oil

¼ small green bell pepper, diced

1 small tomato, deseeded and diced

Plain Omelette (page 64)

1. Heat the oil in a small skillet and fry the bell pepper for a couple of minutes until picking up some color. Add the tomato and cook for another few seconds to warm through, then keep the bell pepper and tomato warm until you are ready to add them to your omelette.

2. Make a Plain Omelette (page 64), and when ready to add additional ingredients to the omelette, add in three-fourths of the pepper and tomato mix.

3. Flip the omelette out and top with the remaining pepper and tomato pieces. You may use tongs to decorate—just be careful not to touch them, as they'll be hot!

OMELETTES ARE THE BEST!

BACON AND BROCCOLI OMELETTE

Prep time: 5 minutes • Cooking time: 10 minutes • Makes 1 omelette

Another popular topping doled out by the Giant Omelette is the Bacon and Broccoli Omelette. This delectable version is teeming with **fiber-friendly broccoli** and **hearty bacon.**

"One of a Skeiths favourite foods, the Bacon and Broccoli Omelette covers all main food groups."

INGREDIENTS

2 strips bacon

¾ cup broccoli

Plain Omelette (page 64)

KIND TIP!

To make this recipe vegetarian, swap the bacon for a plant-based version. You can make vegetarian bacon yourself by charring shiitake mushrooms in an oven with a bit of olive oil, salt, and smoked paprika.

BONUS!

You can eat this omelette until there's only four chunky bits left. Rearrange on a plate for 1/3 Bacon and Broccoli Omelette. *Et voilà!*

1. Heat a small skillet. Fry the bacon until golden and crisp. Lay out some paper towels. Remove the bacon strips from the skillet with tongs and set them on the paper towels. Allow the strips to cool until you can handle them comfortably, then chop them up—this is easiest done with kitchen scissors.

2. Blanch a few small pieces of long-stem or broccoli florets in a pot of boiling water for 3 minutes until cooked but still a little crunchy.

3. Make the Plain Omelette (page 64), and when ready to add additional ingredients to the omelette, tip in three-fourths of the bacon and broccoli.

4. Flip the omelette out and top with the remaining broccoli and bacon. You may use tongs to decorate—just be careful not to touch the broccoli or bacon, as they'll be hot!

SWEET

PYRAMIBREAD

Prep time: 10 minutes • **Makes 1 bread pyramid**

A popular delicacy in **Sakhmet City**, the **Pyramibread** is made to resemble the Pyramids in the **Lost Desert of Neopia**, with a twist–jam, of course! Users love visiting the Lost Desert for **Coltzan's Shrine, Fruit Machine,** and **Sutek's Tomb,** among more.

"A bready pudding with a secret tomb of raspberry jam inside - the revolutionary way to eat bread!"

INGREDIENTS

4 slices white bread
(gluten-free optional)
Raspberry jam, for spreading

1. For the base, take a slice of bread and cut just the crusts off, leaving it as large as possible. Select another piece of bread and cut the crusts off again, this time taking slightly more of the bread with it, so the square is a little smaller. Do this again to get the next layer up.

2. For the final three smaller layers, you can probably get these all out of one piece. Cut the largest square out, and then another two, making it smaller each time. Blend any leftover bread (including crusts) into breadcrumbs for cooking other dishes.

3. Once you have all your layers cut, it's time to make your pyramid. Spread a layer of raspberry jam on the second-to-smallest square, then place it in the middle of the largest square, jam side down. Repeat, spreading the jam on a piece of bread that will sit above the last one, then inverting it and sticking it to the square below, until you have stacked your whole pyramid.

Something has happened!

A passing **DESERT AISHA** says, "Pyramibread pairs nicely with a game of Pyramids. Pyramids is a card game that costs only 50 Neopoints to play, so what are you waiting for?"

BANANA FAELLIE CAKE

Faellies are adorable **faerie petpets** with large, sensitive ears, a swishy tail, and wings. Their kind nature makes them a popular petpet choice. These **Banana Faellie Cakes** play homage to some of *Neopets'* most popular friends, with the Faellie's iconic ears and sweet disposition. Or, as the item's description says...

"Just a faerie cake, only it looks like a Faellie :)"

INGREDIENTS

FOR THE CAKES:

2 bananas

1 stick plus 3 tablespoons or
  ⅔ cup (5 oz./150g) butter,
  melted

¾ cup (5 oz./150g) granulated
  sugar

2 teaspoons vanilla bean paste

2 extra large eggs, beaten

1¾ cups (8 oz./220g)
  all-purpose flour

2 teaspoons baking powder

½ teaspoon baking soda

FOR THE DECORATION:

2 sticks or scant 1 cup
  (7 oz./200g) butter, softened

2¾ cups (14 oz./400g)
  confectioners' sugar

2 teaspoons vanilla extract

Splash of milk

Yellow food coloring

Chocolate ball
  sprinkles

24 long banana
  chips

1. Preheat the oven to 350°F (180°C) and line a 12-hole cupcake tin with cupcake liners.

2. Peel the bananas and place them in a bowl, then purée with a fork. A few small lumps are fine, but try to get most of them out.

3. Stir in the butter, sugar, and vanilla until well combined, then stir in the eggs.

4. Sift the flour into a clean bowl and add the baking powder and baking soda. Add to the mixture and beat briefly until just combined.

5. Spoon the batter equally into the cupcake liners and bake for 20 minutes, or until risen and golden on top. Leave to cool in the tin for a few minutes, then transfer to a wire rack to cool completely.

6. Meanwhile, make the frosting. Beat the butter briefly to loosen it, then add the confectioners' sugar, vanilla, and milk and beat again, until everything is combined and the frosting is light and fluffy. Add just enough yellow food coloring to dye the icing a pale shade of yellow.

7. Spread the icing onto the top of each cupcake, sculpting it slightly with a pallet knife so it rises to a peak at the top. Sprinkle the top with chocolate balls, then insert a pair of banana chip ears, to finish.

Something has happened!

If you visit a Neopet's lookup that has a **FAELLIE** less than 15 days old, you'll get a new Faellie avatar for use at the Neoboards. (Of course, assuming you don't already have it!)

Faellies can be painted a variety of colours at the Petpet Rainbow Pool, like this Blue Faellie.

KIND TIP!

To make this vegan or dairy-free, swap the butter and milk with your favourite plant-based options and use your preferred egg substitute. Flax eggs make a great egg replacement—combine 2 tablespoons of ground flax with 5 tablespoons of water in a bowl, let sit for 5 minutes, mix again, and add to the recipe as you would eggs.

GHOST MARSHMALLOWS

Prep time: 30 minutes • Cooking time: 10 minutes • Makes lots of marshmallows!

These **Ghost Marshmallows** may be spooky, but they also taste great! If you're feeling up for it, you can adjust the Ghost Marshmallows' faces to have different expressions. In **Neopia**, these are regular marshmallows, but if you happen to find some **Magic Ghost Marshmallows**, they'll heal any Ghost-colored **Neopet** to full hit points (which proves helpful if you're a **Battledome** player).

"Hang on, I swear one of these just winked at me..."

INGREDIENTS

2 tablespoons confectioners' sugar

1 tablespoon cornstarch

1 cup (8 fl. oz./250ml) hot (not boiling) water

2 tablespoons (2 packets) gelatin powder

1¾ cups (12 oz./350g) granulated sugar

1 tablespoon liquid glucose or light corn syrup

2 egg whites

1 tablespoon vanilla extract

A brown edible-ink pen

OOOO, SCARY!

1. Grease an 8 by 10-inch (20 by 25-cm) baking tray and line it with parchment paper, leaving some parchment paper overhanging that can be used as a handle to pull the marshmallow from the tray. Combine the confectioners' sugar and cornstarch in a small bowl, then dust the mixture all over the lined tray and set aside. Keep any leftover sugar mixture to use when cutting out.

2. Pour ½ cup (4 fl. oz./125ml) of the hot water into a small bowl or cup and sprinkle the gelatin into it. Stir, then leave it to dissolve while you make the syrup, stirring occasionally.

3. Reserve 1 tablespoon of the sugar in a small bowl. Place the remaining ½ cup hot water in a saucepan with the remaining sugar and the liquid glucose. Place the pan over medium heat and stir until the sugar is dissolved, then cook without stirring (although you can swirl the pan to avoid any hot spots) until it forms a syrup—you need it to register 248°F (120°C) on a candy thermometer, so it will take a few minutes to get to this temperature. At this point, remove it from the heat and leave to cool for a few minutes while you prepare the eggs.

4. Place the egg whites into the bowl of a stand mixer fitted with a whisk attachment. Whisk until soft peaks form, then add the 1 tablespoon of sugar and whisk until you have stiff peaks.

5. Stir the gelatin mixture and vanilla extract into the syrup until combined. Now, with the whisk running, pour the syrup into the egg mixture, making sure to pour it down the side of the bowl rather than into the beaters, which could splatter the mixture straight back out at you. Once all the syrup is added, keep whisking for 5 minutes until the mixture is almost cool and firming up.

6. Pour the marshmallow into the prepared tin and pop it in the fridge for 2 to 3 hours to set.

7. Once the marshmallow is set, lift it out of the tray using the overhanging parchment. Using a cookie cutter (or a sharp knife) that you have dusted with the cornstarch and sugar mixture, cut out your ghost shapes. As you cut them, roll the freshly cut sides in the cornstarch mixture to stop them from being so sticky.

8. Using the edible-ink pen, draw little faces onto your ghosts.

FLORAL JELLY

Some **Neopians** think **Jelly World** is a myth–however, keen-eyed players know how to get to the **Jelly Blobs of Doom**, the **Giant Jelly**, **Bouncy Supreme**, and more. Perhaps most popular in Jelly World, however, is a **Giant Jelly** that's guarded by the **Jelly Keeper** and bestows one helping of jelly per day, per player. Although this **Floral Jelly** is a tad rarer on-site, it makes a fantastic meal for your **Neopian** friends. After all...

"It's jelly with flowers inside...made of jelly!"

INGREDIENTS

¼ pack each of yellow, blue, red, green, and pink gelatin, like Jell-O

2 packets unflavored gelatin (or enough to set 4 cups/2 pints water)

½ cup (3½ oz./100g) granulated sugar

Violet or purple food coloring

Good-quality violet extract

EQUIPMENT:

Silicone flower molds

1. Start by making the flowers. Mix up all the colored gelatin (in separate bowls) at twice the intended concentration, i.e., put half as much water in as directed on the packages. This will help the flowers set more firmly so they are much less likely to break when being removed from the molds. Pour the gelatin into the molds and leave in the refrigerator to set until firm.

2. Place the gelatin and sugar in a heatproof pitcher and pour in 4¼ cups (35 fl. oz./1L) of hot water. Stir until the sugar is dissolved, then add a couple of drops of purple food coloring to tint the liquid a pale-violet color. Don't add too much; if this gelatin base is too dark, you won't be able to see the flowers very well. Add a few drops of violet extract, tasting and adding a little more as you go, until you get the strength of flavor you prefer. Allow the liquid to cool completely but not set. (If you rush this, you may melt your flowers.)

3. Find yourself a 6-inch round nonstick cake pan with a nondetachable base (or the gelatin will run out). Remove the flowers from the molds and place them, detail side down, to cover the base of the pan.

4. Pour a tiny bit of the violet gelatin into the pan to almost cover the flowers. Place the pan in the fridge for 10 minutes so this thin layer can set—this will hold the flowers in place so that they won't float away once you add the rest of the gelatin.

5. Once the first layer has set, remove the pan from the fridge and pour in the remaining violet gelatin. Place it back in the fridge for a least 2 to 3 hours until set completely. Now your jelly is almost complete!

6. To serve the jelly, fill the sink with warm water. Dunk the pan into the water, being careful not to let the water flow over the top, to slightly melt the sides and loosen the jelly. Place a serving plate upside down on top of the tin and invert the plate and tin together so the jelly is transferred to the plate. Now admire your work before you enjoy!

Something has happened!

A passing **PLUSHIE KACHEEK** says, "Violet flavour extract is available online or in specialist baking stores."

KIND TIP!

To make two-tone flowers, you just pour in one layer of colour, let it set, then do another layer in a different colour. You will need graduated molds to do this.

77

NEOPIA BROWNIES

Prep time: 50 minutes • Cooking time: 25 minutes • Makes 9 to 16 brownies

With a fudgy chocolate and nutty core, these **Neopia Brownies** are made to resemble Neopia, of course. There's **sweet blue fondant** for the Neopian waters and Maraqua, as well as the lush green lands of Altador, Roo Island, and Neopia Central, and the snowcapped area of Terror Mountain.

"Delicious chocolate fudge brownies with nuts in them. YUM!"

INGREDIENTS

7 ounces (200g) dark chocolate (70 percent cocoa solids)

6 ounces (175g) butter

¾ cup (75g) ground almonds

Scant ½ cup (75g) all-purpose flour

1½ ounces (40g) cocoa powder

½ teaspoon baking powder

Pinch of sea salt

1 cup plus 2 tablespoons (8 oz./220g) sugar

3 large eggs

3 ounces (85g) pecans, roughly chopped

THE DECORATION:

¼ cup (50g) confectioners' sugar, plus extra for dusting

5½ ounces (150g) blue fondant icing

1¾ ounces (50g) green fondant icing

1. Preheat the oven to 340°F (170°C). Line an 8-inch (20cm) square brownie tin with parchment paper.

2. Place the chocolate and butter into a large heatproof bowl and set over a pan of simmering water, making sure the water doesn't touch the base of the bowl. Leave to melt for a few minutes, stirring occasionally.

3. Meanwhile, combine the almonds, flour, cocoa powder, baking powder, and sea salt in a bowl and set aside.

4. Once melted, add the sugar to the chocolate mixture and stir in, then beat in the eggs. Fold the dry ingredients into the chocolate until almost all combined, then add in the pecans and finish folding everything together.

Continues on next page!

Something has happened!

A **RED NIMMO** says, "In Neopia, there are 54 species of Neopets and over 20 lands, although new lands and Neopets—like Vandagyres—come out of hiding every few years!"

NEOPIA

5. Pour the mixture into the prepared baking pan and bake for about 25 minutes, or until set but still a little bit raw in the middle. It will set as it cools down and be lovely and gooey.

6. Once cooled, you can add your Neopia map! Dust a work surface with the confectioners' sugar and roll out your blue fondant to a square the size of your brownie. You can trim the edges with a knife to get a nice straight edge. Lift the fondant onto the brownie and smooth it over. It will seal itself on after a few minutes, but if you want to feel like you are sticking it down, you could brush the top of the brownie with a little water first.

7. Roll out the green fondant and cut out wonky shapes that look like land masses and islands. Apply them one at a time, painting the back of them with water as you go, to build up your map.

8. Finally, mix your confectioners' sugar with a little water until it is a piping consistency. Spoon it into a piping bag fitted with a small tip and pipe on your icebergs between the land masses.

9. Slice your brownie into 9 or 16 squares to serve.

Neopia. What a lovely planet. I think I'll take it.

KIND TIP!

To make this nut-free, swap the almonds for chocolate chips or simply omit.

MEEPIT JUICE BREAK ICE LOLLY

Feed all the **Meepits** in your life—no tricky pipes needed—with these **Meepit Juice Break Ice Lollies!** Just make sure to feed the **Meepits** before the timer runs out. Otherwise, things can get pretty nasty. Trust us!

"Three tasty juice flavours in one ice lolly!"

INGREDIENTS

1 large chunk watermelon

About ¾ cup (180ml) lemonade

Blue food coloring

About ¾ cup (180ml) orange juice

EQUIPMENT:

A set of six ⅓-cup (90 ml) ice pop molds and wooden sticks

1. Chop the skin off the watermelon and cut it roughly into chunks. Place the flesh in a food processor and blend to a pulp. Set a fine-mesh strainer over a pitcher and tip the pulp into it. Let the juice drain through, then discard the pulp. You will need about ¾ cup (180ml) of the juice. Fill each ice pop mold one-third full, then place the molds in the freezer for 2 to 3 hours until frozen.

2. Pour the lemonade into a pitcher and mix in enough food coloring to get a lovely bright-blue color. Divide it among the ice pop molds, then return the molds to the freezer for 1 hour until starting to set. Once the blue layer is starting to freeze, place a stick in each ice pop (or lolly) and it should stand upright. Return to the freezer until the layer is frozen completely.

3. Finally, top the molds up with your orange juice and return to the freezer to freeze solid.

4. Dip the molds in warm water to release the lolly, then remove from the mold and serve immediately.

> If you prefer Meepit Juice over Meepit Juice Lollies, make each drink separately, do not freeze, and serve in a tall glass—or an old pipe (just like in the game)!

Something has happened!

A **MEEPIT** "meeps" at you. Then it backs away.

ICED FISH CAKE

Prep time: 1¼ hours • Cooking time: 25 minutes • Makes 8 to 10 servings

Although classified as a "Gross Food" by **Neopian** chefs, enjoy our version of **Iced Fish Cake** made with sugary green fish. (Or skip the sugar and go with fish—just don't tell any **Kois**, please.)

"A large fish cake coated in extra sweet strawberry icing. Yum?"

INGREDIENTS

FOR THE ICING:

1¼ cups (200g) confectioners' sugar, plus extra for dusting

Green fondant rolling icing

Black food coloring

Blue food coloring

Large googly (edible) eyes

About 1¾ ounces (50g) strawberries

FOR THE CAKE:

1 cup (250g) butter

1 cup (250g) sugar

5 eggs

6 tablespoons (90ml) milk

1 tablespoon vanilla extract

1¾ cups (250g) self-rising flour

½ teaspoon baking powder

Red food coloring

½ cup strawberry jam

EQUIPMENT:

2 red-and-white-striped candles with holders

Skewers (if necessary)

A grey serving plate

> I think this cake is best eaten by the Healing Springs.

1. The day before you want to decorate the cake, make the green fish, as they will need to dry and harden. Photocopy or trace the template on page 120. Lightly dust a work surface with confectioners' sugar and roll out the fondant to about ¼ inch (½cm) thick (it needs to be thicker than usual to stand up). Draw around the template to mark out one fish, then flip it over and do the same to get another fish pointing the other way. Insert a candleholder into the mouth of each fish and set them on a wire rack so they dry more quickly.

2. Mix a quarter of the confectioners' sugar with a little water to make an icing of pipeable consistency. Divide it evenly into two portions and dye one bowl black and another bowl blue using the food coloring. Transfer the black icing into a piping bag with a very small tip and use it to pipe gills onto the fish. Pipe a blob of icing where the eye will be and set a googly eye on top to stick it on. Put the blue icing into another piping bag with a tiny nozzle and use it to pipe the lips on the fish, then leave them on the wire rack overnight to set hard.

3. Preheat the oven to 350°F (180°C). Grease two 8-inch (20-cm) cake pans and line the base and sides with parchment paper.

Continues on next page!

KIND TIP!

If you can't find large googly eyes, you can make them with a ball of white fondant icing that you press to flatten a little, then pipe a black dot in the middle, using the same icing you use for the gills.

4. To make the cake, place the butter and sugar in a stand mixer (or into a large mixing bowl if you're using an electric hand whisk) and cream together until pale and fluffy.

5. In a bowl, lightly beat the eggs with the milk and vanilla extract. Sift the flour and baking powder into another bowl.

6. Add half the egg mixture to the butter and beat it in, then add half the flour mixture. Repeat to incorporate everything, then quickly beat in enough red food coloring to dye the batter a dark-pink shade.

7. Divide the batter evenly between the prepared pans and bake for about 25 minutes, or until risen and a skewer inserted into the center of the cakes comes out clean. Leave to cool in the pans for a few minutes before turning out onto a wire rack to cool completely.

8. Once the cakes are cool, level the tops with a sharp knife, if necessary. Place one cake on the serving plate and spread the strawberry jam over the top. Place the other cake on top. Using a sharp knife, dig two channels across the middle line of the cake, each the same width as a fish. Slot the fish in to check they fit (and these will help them stand up).

9. To make the icing, place the strawberries in a mini blender or the small bowl of a food processor and blend to a puree. Strain the pulp through a sieve to extract the juice. Place the remaining confectioners' sugar in a bowl and pour in enough of the juice to make a thick icing; go slowly, as you will only need about 1 to 1½ tablespoons. Spread the icing over the top of the cake, letting it run down the sides a little. Locate the slits you have cut and insert a fish into each one, then leave to set. Before serving, insert a candle into each candleholder and light it up!

FONDANT IS GOOD. FONDANT IS GREAT. HAHA.

ORANGE CLOUD COOKIE

Prep time: 45 minutes • Cooking time: 1¹/₂ hours • Makes 12 cookies

These **Orange Cloud Cookies** are a delightful Faerie Food. They are light and chewy with an orange-flavored cream center. However, if you prefer a different flavor, simply swap the orange extract for strawberry.

"An orange treat that wont spoil your appetite."

INGREDIENTS

FOR THE COOKIES:

4 extra-large egg whites

1 cup (7 oz./200g) superfine sugar

FOR THE FILLING:

¾ cup plus 2 tablespoons (200ml) heavy cream

Orange food coloring

1 teaspoon orange extract

3 tablespoons confectioners' sugar

1. Preheat the oven to 230°F (110°C) and line two large baking sheets with parchment paper.

2. To make your meringue, you need to start with a perfectly clean and grease-free mixing bowl and whisk (or stand mixer and whisk attachment). Place your egg whites in the bowl and whisk to soft peaks, then start adding the sugar, a spoonful at a time, whisking the sugar in well before you add the next spoonful. Once all the sugar is added, keep whisking for a few minutes until the meringue is stiff and glossy. When you rub a bit of it between your thumb and forefinger, it shouldn't feel grainy at all.

3. Spoon the meringue into a piping bag fitted with a large, round nozzle. Pipe fingers of meringue, folding the meringue over on itself as you go to form a fluffy cloud effect. Try to make them all the same length so they match up when it comes to sandwiching the cookies—you could draw guidelines on the parchment paper first if you like. You should be able to make about 24 clouds—12 per sheet. Place the sheets in the oven and turn the heat down to 200°F (100°C). Cook for 1½ hours, then turn the heat off and allow the meringue clouds to cool down in the oven.

4. Once the meringues are cool, you can make your orange cream. Place the cream in a bowl and color it to a bright-orange shade with food coloring. Add the orange flavoring and confectioner's sugar too. Using a balloon whisk, whisk the cream until soft peaks form. Be very careful not to go too far—it should still be quite soft and shouldn't look grainy at all. Use a spatula to spread a good amount onto a cookie and then sandwich it together with another cookie. Repeat to fill and sandwich 12 cookies.

THESE COOKIES ARE NATURALLY NUT-FREE AND MAKE GREAT LUNCHBOX SNACKS.

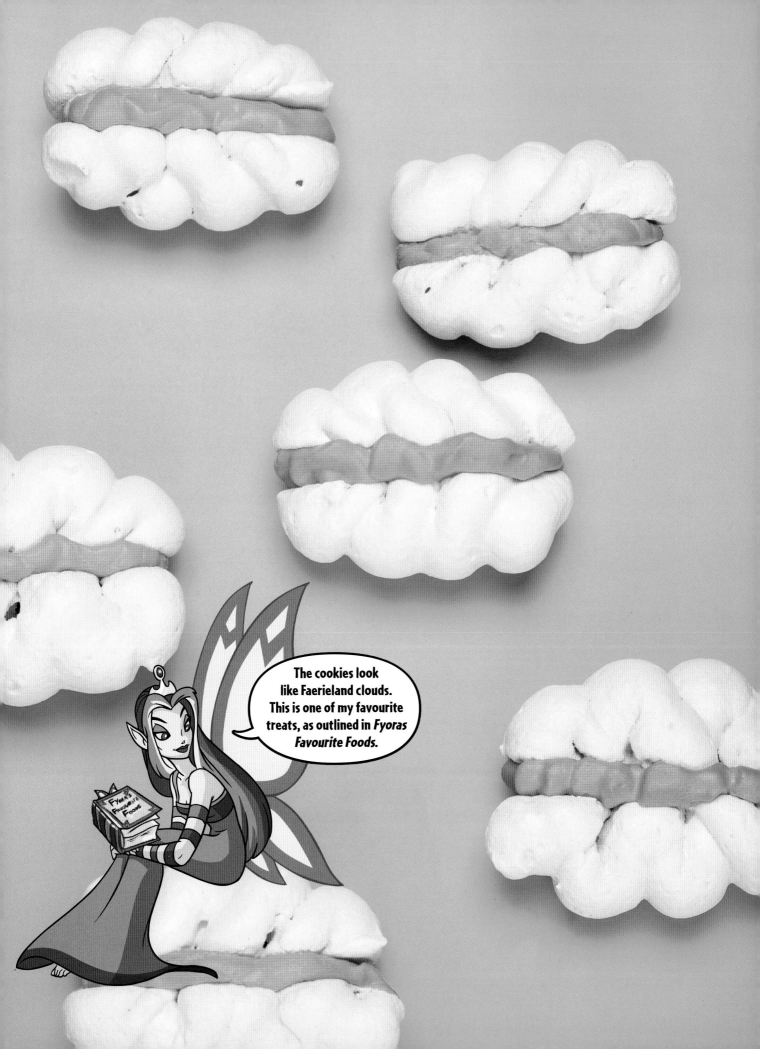

GHOSTMALLOW SMORE

Prep time: 5 minutes • Cooking time: 10 minutes • Makes 4 smores

For a **Neopian** take on a summer classic, try out this **Ghostmallow Smore**, which is sure to be a new favorite. When made in a batch like below, they're spectacularly spooky with the right amount of sweet. Included are directions for cooks with grills and cooks without them—we don't judge.

"Mmmmm... chocolate, graham crackers and ghostmallows."

INGREDIENTS

8 chocolate graham crackers

2 to 3 squares of milk chocolate per smore

8 Ghost Marshmallows (page 74)

KIND TIP!

Use gluten-free graham crackers if following a gluten-free diet. You can also use dark chocolate instead of milk for a dairy-free version.

1. If you have a barbeque or grill with coals, lay out four sheets of aluminum foil. Place a graham cracker on each sheet and top with 2 to 3 squares of chocolate. Add a Ghost Marshmallow on top and finish with another cracker. Repeat to assemble all four smores.

2. Wrap the foil sheets around the smores and place them in the ashes of a cooling barbeque. Leave them until the chocolate and marshmallow have melted—the length of time will depend on how hot your ashes are, so just keep checking (carefully—they're hot!) until the smores are as gooey as you desire, then gorge on them.

ALTERNATE METHOD:

If you are indoors, this is still totally achievable! Preheat your broiler to medium-high. Line a broiler pan (or grill pan) with foil—this will save a lot of cleaning!—and lay out your first four crackers. Add the chocolate squares on top and place the pan under the broiler for a few minutes until the chocolate is softened and melting. Add the marshmallows on top and return the pan to the broiler. Cook until the marshmallows are melting and beginning to brown on top. Place the remaining crackers on top and indulge in the same manner as if you were outside.

Delightfully sweet. Just how I like them.

WHATEVER YOU SAY, JHUDORA!

KRAWK PAW COOKIE

Krawks are the rarest **Neopet** in all **Neopia**, because they can only be created in the **Fungus Cave** of **Krawk Island** (or by transforming another Neopet with a **Morphing Potion**). These **Krawk Paw Cookies** are made to resemble the elusive Neopet's paws. Then they're covered with hundreds and thousands of sprinkles–or however many you'd like!

"A freshly baked cookie shaped like a Krawks paw with hundreds and thousands sprinkles on top."

INGREDIENTS

FOR THE COOKIES:

⅔ cup (5½ oz./150g) butter, softened

¾ cup (5½ oz./150g) granulated sugar

1 egg

1 teaspoon vanilla bean paste or vanilla extract

2¼ cups (10 oz./300g) all-purpose flour, plus extra for dusting

1 teaspoon baking powder

FOR THE DECORATION:

1½ cups (10½ oz./300g) confectioners' sugar

Green food coloring

Sugar sprinkles (nonpareils)

1. To make the cookies, place the butter and sugar in a stand mixer fitted with a paddle attachment and beat until light and fluffy.

2. Add the egg and vanilla bean paste and continue to beat until well combined.

3. Firmly but quickly mix in the flour and baking powder and bring it together into a ball. Be careful not to overmix, as it may make the cookies tough. Flatten the dough into a large patty, wrap it in plastic wrap, and chill for at least 30 minutes.

4. While the dough chills, preheat the oven to 350°F (180°C) and line two large baking sheets with parchment paper. Photocopy or trace the template on page 120 and cut it out.

5. Dust a work surface with a little flour and roll out the dough to about ⅛ inch (2 to 3mm) thick. Place the template over the dough and draw around it with a sharp knife to cut out your Krawk Paw Cookies. Get as many as you can out of the rolled sheet, then gather up the excess dough and reroll it to make more. Lay as many cookies as you can on the baking sheets and bake for about 9 minutes, or until pale golden. Leave to cool on the baking sheets for a few minutes, then transfer to wire racks to cool completely while you bake the next batch.

6. Once all the cookies are baked and cooled, you can decorate. Place the confectioners' sugar in a bowl and add about 2 tablespoons of water, a little at a time, until you have a thick icing. Add enough green food coloring to make it an attractive Krawk green, then spread it over the cookies. No need to be too neat here—Krawks are not the most elegant creatures! Scatter the sprinkles over the cookies and leave to set before enjoying your little monsters.

Something has happened!

A **CAMOUFLAGE KRAWK** comes out of hiding and says, "Krawks are both Neopets and Petpets. We are not, however, Petpetpets."

HALF RAINBOW JELLY

This jelly has all the flavor of the rainbow–divided in half, of course. The colors of this jelly are quite vibrant and beautiful and look great at birthday parties or Pride celebrations. Rainbow is also a color that your **Neopet** can be painted, and there are over five hundred other rainbow items on the *Neopets* website. Personally, we like to enjoy this **Half Rainbow Jelly** on a **Rainbow Cybunny Chair**.

"Oh dear it looks like someone has already eaten part of this jelly"

INGREDIENTS

¼ pack each gelatin (like Jell-O) in all the colors of the rainbow!

WE SUGGEST USING THE FOLLOWING FLAVORS:

Red layer—strawberry

Orange layer—orange, of course (or peach)

Yellow layer—lemon

Green layer—lime

Blue layer—blueberry

Indigo layer—black cherry or black currant

1. First, mix up your red gelatin following the proportions on the packet. You will only need about one-fourth of a packet, so just mix it with ¼ of the hot water quantity stated. Pour it into a classic-shaped gelatin mold and place in the fridge to set.

2. Once the red layer is set, repeat this process with the orange gelatin, letting the liquid cool before you pour it in, or it may start to melt the set gelatin below. Continue, mixing up and setting all the different colored gelatins in the order listed in the ingredients list. Chill again until ready to serve.

3. Now your jelly is almost complete. To serve, fill the sink with warm water. Dunk the tin into the water, being careful not to let the water flow over the top, to slightly melt the sides and loosen the jelly. Place a serving plate upside down on top of the tin and invert the plate and tin together so the jelly is transferred to the plate.

4. Chop the jelly in half and remove one half (what you do with that half is up to you—donate it, eat it quickly before guests arrive, or maybe stick it in the fridge for later). Serve on a violet plate. Voilà!

Something has happened!

A passing **RAINBOW HISSI** says, "As the jelly mold gets wider toward the base, you will get thinner layers of jelly. If you're a purist and want to make sure each layer is the same depth, divide the height of the tin equally into six, then measure this distance repeatedly up the inside of the tin, making a small mark each time with an edible-ink pen. Pour in the red jelly until you hit this mark and then stop and let it set as before. Pour in the next colour of jelly until you hit the next mark and continue until you have added all the colours and reach the top of the tin. You will have leftover jelly this way—just pour it into separate bowls or mugs to enjoy whenever."

WHITE CHOCOLATE GRARRL TEETH

Prep time: 10 minutes, plus chilling • Cooking time: 10 minutes • Makes lots!

Perhaps no Neopet has a bigger appetite than a **Grarrl**. If a Grarrl is very hungry, famished, or dying of hunger, they might eat anything–and we do mean *anything*–from your inventory. They are perhaps only rivaled by **Skeiths**, but we'd rather not see that fight break out.

"A fudgy chocolate treat that looks very similar to Grarrl teeth."

INGREDIENTS

- 17 ounces (480g) white chocolate, broken into small chunks
- 1 14-ounce (397g) can sweetened condensed milk
- 2 tablespoons butter
- 2½ ounces (75g) blanched hazelnuts, finely chopped

1. Line a 2-pound loaf pan with parchment paper.

2. Place the chocolate, condensed milk, and butter in a large saucepan. Cook over medium-low heat, stirring until everything has melted and incorporated. Continue cooking for 2 to 3 minutes, then add the hazelnuts and stir in well.

3. Pour the mixture into the prepared pan and spread level, then chill for a few hours or overnight, until set.

4. Once set, slice lengthwise on the diagonal. Cut these into small pyramids in the shape of fang-like teeth. Keep in the fridge.

Something has happened!

A **GREEN TONU** passes by and says, "Did you know? Grarrls are native to Tyrannia, a prehistoric land located far under the surface of Neopia. One of the most famous Grarrls is Grarrg, the Tyrannian Battle Master in the Battledome."

KIND TIP!

If looking for a nut-free version, simply omit or swap the hazelnuts for puffed rice.

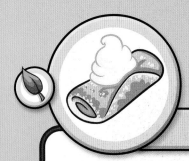

MAPLE CREPE WITH CREAM

Prep time: 5 minutes • Cooking time: 20 minutes • Makes 8 to 10 crepes

This Neopian baked good is a favorite. If you're lucky, you might find it alongside **Harfell Mince Pie** and **French Onion Soup Cake** at **The Bakery**. We like pairing this maple dish with **Sliced Strawberries**, although it's also delicious eaten on its own.

"A freshly baked crepe flavoured with maple sugar and topped with fresh cream."

INGREDIENTS

¾ cup (4¼ oz./120g) all-purpose flour

Pinch of salt

2 eggs

Scant 1 cup (7 fl. oz./200ml) semi-skim milk mixed with 5 tablespoons water

3 tablespoons butter, plus extra for greasing the pan

Maple sugar, to sprinkle

1¼ cups (10½ fl. oz./300ml) heavy cream, whipped

Sliced strawberries, to serve (optional)

1. Sift the flour into a bowl, add the salt, and make a well in the middle. Crack in the eggs and whisk gently with a balloon whisk to beat them and start incorporating the flour. Add the milk and water and continue to whisk until you have a smooth batter.

2. Find a crepe pan or similar-sized shallow-sided frying pan and set it over medium heat. Add the butter and melt it, then add it to the batter and stir in. This will also grease your pan ready for the first crepe.

3. Ladle a little of the batter into the prepared pan and swirl it around to thinly coat the base of the pan. You don't want your pancakes to be too thick, but the first one is generally sacrificial—to judge how much batter you need for the remaining ones! Let it cook for a minute or so until set and beginning to turn lightly golden on the bottom, then flip it over—with a spatula or by jolting the pan, depending on how brave you are feeling—and cooking for a few seconds on the other side.

4. Tip the crepe onto a plate and sprinkle with maple sugar. Roll up and finish with a blob of cream and the strawberries if you like. Repeat to cook all the batter.

> Neopets love crepes. If you prefer a different flavour, try out a Delicious Borovan Crepe, with Borovan piled on top.

CHOCOLATE DOUGHNUTFRUIT

Prep time: 40 minutes, plus proofing • Cooking time: 20 minutes • Makes 12

Doughnutfruits are sweet fruits that look like doughnuts. Of course, since these don't naturally grow on non-Neopian lands, we think our (mostly) doughnut version is delicious. Doughnutfruits can commonly be found when playing the game **Hassee Bounce.**

"Even more delicious than a normal Doughnutfruit. This was a prize from the Advent Calendar in Y6."

INGREDIENTS

- 7 tablespoons (3½ fl. oz./ 100ml) whole milk
- 1 tablespoon (12g) sugar
- ¼-ounce (7-g) packet dried fast-action yeast
- 3½ tablespoons (1¾ oz./50g) butter
- 1 egg, beaten
- 1 teaspoon vanilla extract
- 1⅔ cups (7¾ oz./220g) strong white bread flour, plus extra for dusting
- 4 tablespoons cocoa powder
- Pinch of salt
- 1 quart sunflower or peanut oil for deep-frying, plus a drizzle for greasing the bowl
- ¾ cup (3½ oz./100g) confectioners' sugar

1. Warm the milk for about 20 seconds in the microwave. You only need it lukewarm, or it may kill the yeast (added next). Stir in the sugar and the yeast, then set aside for a few minutes until the top gets frothy.

2. Meanwhile, melt the butter in a bowl in the microwave for about 20 seconds and set aside to cool. Once no longer hot, whisk in the egg, vanilla extract, and the yeast-milk mixture.

3. Sift the flour into the bowl of a stand mixer or into a large mixing bowl. Add 2 tablespoons of the cocoa powder and the salt. Make a well in the middle and pour in the butter and yeast mixture. Knead with a dough hook for about 5 minutes until smooth and elastic, or stir together with a spoon, then tip out onto a work surface and knead by hand for about 10 minutes.

4. Grease a clean bowl with a little oil and pop the dough in. Cover and leave to rise for about 45 minutes, or until doubled in size. In the meantime, line two baking sheets with nonstick baking parchment.

Continues on next page!

Something has happened!

A **SPECKLED ACARA** scurries over and says, "If you prefer, you can add pink frosting and sprinkles to the Doughnutfruit for a Sprinkled Doughnutfruit!"

5. Once risen, knead the dough briefly to expel the air, then divide it into 12 even portions. Roll each portion into a ball, then roll it flat on a lightly floured surface until you have a rough circle about ½ inch (1cm) thick. It doesn't matter if they're a bit wobbly or more elongated and oval shaped—doughnutfruit are irregular shapes! Use a 1¼ inch (3cm) round cookie cutter to stamp out a hole from the middle. Transfer the doughnut to a prepared baking tray, reserving the hole you have cut out. Repeat to shape all 12 doughnutfruit, spacing them well apart on the trays. Grease the tops of them by brushing with a little oil, then cover with plastic wrap. Fill a large saucepan half full with oil and heat it to 350°F (180°C).

6. Take one of the small hole pieces you cut out from the center of a doughnut and roll it out a little. Stamp out a small star using a 1½ inch (4-cm) star cookie cutter, or shape with your hands. Pinch the points of the star a little more to flatten and elongate them, then drop the star into the hot oil. Leave to cook for about 30 seconds, then fish out the star with a slotted spoon and leave to drain on a plate lined with paper towels. Repeat to cook 12 small misshapen stars (you can cook a few at a time if you remember which order to fish them out in), which will be the stalks of your fruit.

7. Once your stalks are cooked, cook a batch of two or three doughnuts at a time, carefully lowering each doughnut into the oil using the slotted spoon. Fry for about 45 seconds on each side or until crisp and deep brown. Fish them out with the slotted spoon and leave to drain on paper towels. Repeat to cook all 12 doughnuts.

8. Once your doughnuts have cooled, mix the confectioners' sugar and the remaining 2 tablespoons of cocoa powder with a tiny bit of water—just enough so that you have a thick icing of pipeable consistency. Transfer the icing to a piping bag with a very small tip and pipe a zigzag line of icing all around the top of the ring, finishing with a larger blob. Place a small star doughnut on the blob and leave to set and adhere before serving.

MONEY TREE CUPCAKE

Prep time: 40 minutes • Cooking time: 20 minutes • Makes 12 cucpakes

In *Neopets*, these cupcakes *technically* aren't food—they're **wearable!** However, in our version, you can eat them (or wear them—no judgement) to celebrate the **Money Tree**, a friendly tree at the heart of **Neopia** where **kind-hearted souls** can donate items and Neopoints to those in need.

"This delicious cupcake is green like the Money Tree! This is a super food that will fill your Neopet up to a bloated state and make it happier!"

INGREDIENTS

FOR THE CUPCAKES:

⅔ cup (170ml) vegetable or safflower oil

2 eggs

½ cup (4 fl. oz./125ml) milk

1½ cup (180g) self-rising flour

5 tablespoons (1½ oz./40g) cocoa powder

½ teaspoon baking soda

1 teaspoon baking powder

¾ cup plus 1 tablespoon (160g) granulated sugar

Pinch of salt

FOR THE DECORATION:

2 sticks or 1 cup and 1 table-spoon (250g) butter

2¼ cups (500g) confectioners' sugar

2 teaspoons vanilla extract

4 to 5 tablespoons milk

Green food coloring

24 chocolate-covered pretzels

Gold ball sprinkles

1. Preheat the oven to 350°F (180°C) and line a 12-hole muffin pan with cupcake cups.

2. In a large mixing bowl, whisk together the oil, eggs, and milk.

3. Sift the flour and cocoa powder into another bowl and stir in the baking soda, baking powder, sugar, and salt.

4. Add the dry ingredients to the wet ones and fold everything together quickly.

5. Divide the batter evenly among the cupcake liners, filling them about two-thirds full. Bake for 18 to 20 minutes, until well risen. Leave them to cool in the tin for a few minutes, then transfer them to a wire rack to cool completely.

6. Once cool, you can decorate your trees. Place the butter, confectioners' sugar, and vanilla extract into the bowl of a stand mixer with a balloon whisk attachment (or into a large mixing bowl if you are using an electric hand whisk) and beat until light and fluffy. Give this a good amount of time until it is really whipped up. You might have to stop the machine and scrape down the sides with a spatula from time to time. Add the milk until you have a smooth frosting that's a slightly looser, pipeable consistency, then add the green food coloring to dye it green.

7. Spoon the frosting into a piping bag fitted with a large star tip and pipe a swirl of frosting on the top of each cupcake.

8. Carefully cut off the two loops of each pretzel, so you are left with just the "Y" shaped piece in the middle. Dip the tips of the "Y" into any spare icing (there's usually a little bit left in the piping bag that won't pipe easily) to give the trunk leaves, then stick two trees in the top of each cupcake. Finish the cakes with a few gold balls and enjoy.

Something has happened!

A **Coconut JubJub** says, "Balthazar, a Bounty Hunting Lupe, often makes donations to the Money Tree. Those donations are usually bottled Faeries."

GREY WAFFLES

Rumor has it these waffles are the Grey Faerie's favorite breakfast. Served with grey syrup or cookies-and-cream whipped cream, these just might become your favorite breakfast too.

"Pass the grey syrup?"

INGREDIENTS

FOR THE WAFFLES:

1¼ cups (170g) all-purpose flour

1 teaspoon baking powder

¼ teaspoon baking soda

1 tablespoon granulated sugar

2 large eggs

Scant 1 cup (8 fl. oz./225ml) milk

¼ cup (2 oz./60g) butter, melted, plus extra for greasing

½ tablespoon vanilla bean paste or vanilla extract

Black food coloring

FOR THE GREY SYRUP:

½ cup (100g) white sugar

1 tablespoon vanilla extract

Black food coloring

1. First, get your grey syrup cooking, as this will take a few minutes. Put the sugar in a small saucepan with 4 tablespoons water. Stir until the sugar is dissolved, then cook over low-medium heat for a few minutes until thickened a little. Stir in the vanilla extract and enough black food coloring to make it grey.

2. For the waffles, sift the flour, baking powder, and baking soda into a large mixing bowl and stir in the sugar.

3. In another bowl, whisk together the eggs, milk, butter, and vanilla, then add this to the dry ingredients and whisk everything together. Add enough black food coloring to make the waffles a deep-grey color.

4. Leave the batter to rest while you preheat your waffle maker to medium heat and grease it with a little melted butter.

5. Pour enough batter into the waffle maker to almost fill it and close the lid. Cook for 4 to 5 minutes, or follow the manufacturer's instructions, until the waffle is risen and crisp on the outside.

6. Keep the waffles warm in a low oven while you cook the rest of the waffles.

7. Serve the grey waffles topped with the grey syrup.

CANTALOUPE SLUSHIE

Prep time: 15 minutes, plus freezing • Makes 1 to 2 servings

Cantaloupe lovers, rejoice! This one's for you. Most **Neopian slushies** can be found at the **Slushie Shop**, which is overseen by a **Striped Eyrie** on **Terror Mountain**. Slushies taste best in the winter!

"Fans of melon flavours should enjoy this slushie!"

INGREDIENTS

1 cantaloupe

1 to 2 tablespoons granulated sugar (optional)

EQUIPMENT:

A clear takeout cup with a domed lid and a straw

1. Deseed and peel the cantaloupe and place it into a blender or food processor. Blend until it is smooth, then pour it through a fine-mesh strainer to get rid of the solids. Push it around in the strainer with a spoon to make sure you extract as much juice as possible, then discard what's in the strainer. Add sugar to taste and stir to dissolve. Pour the juice into a shallow container, such as a wide ice cream tub or deep tray, and place in the freezer until frozen solid.

2. When you are ready to serve, dunk your container into a sink of warm water to defrost the bottom and free your cantaloupe ice block. It doesn't matter if it starts to melt a bit—you want that, as the liquid will help you blend it all up. Break up the block, pop it all in a food processor, and blend it to a mush. You can wait for it to melt a little more to get to slushie consistency, or if you're feeling impatient, just scoop out a big spoonful of the ice and microwave it until you have a lukewarm juice, then blend it back in.

3. Pour into 1 large takeout cup (or two smaller glasses) and add a straw to serve.

If cantaloupe isn't your favourite flavour, you can swap for a whole cheeseburger. I don't recommend feeding Cheeseburger Slushies to Skeiths, though. It gives them a curious case of the Neezles. Rather, I recommend Skeith Burgers, which you can find on page 44.

ILLUSEN BISCOTTI

Prep time: 30 minutes • Cooking time: 1 hour • Makes about 24 cookies

Illusen is an **Earth Faerie** who dwells in **Meridell**. She is one of the most beloved Faeries in all Neopia, and there's even a day—**Illusen Day**—to celebrate her. You can enjoy this **Illusen Biscotti** whenever you please. Just maybe don't tell Illusen's archnemesis, the Dark Faerie **Jhudora.**

"Crispy bread with herbs and [and] spices baked right in."

INGREDIENTS

- ¾ cup plus 1 teaspoon (120g) pistachio nuts
- 1¾ cups (8 oz./225g) all-purpose flour
- 1 cup plus 2 tablespoons (4½ oz./125g) soft light-brown sugar
- 1½ teaspoons baking powder
- 1½ teaspoons ground cardamom
- ¼ teaspoon dried thyme
- 2 tablespoons cocoa powder
- Pinch of salt
- 2 eggs
- 2 ounces (60g) dark chocolate chips

1. Preheat the oven to 340°F (170°C) and line a baking sheet with parchment paper.

2. Select 2 ounces (60g) of the greenest pistachios and set them aside, then place the rest into a mini chopper, a spice grinder, or the small bowl of a food processor and blend to a fine powder.

3. Combine the ground pistachios, flour, sugar, baking powder, cardamom, thyme, cocoa powder, and salt in the bowl of a stand mixer. Add the eggs and mix until everything looks evenly mixed. It will look very dry at first but soon will start to clump together. At this point, add the whole pistachios and chocolate chips and mix again briefly to distribute evenly.

4. Bring the dough together with your hands and roll it into a long sausage shape, about 12 inches (30cm) long. Transfer it to the baking sheet and bake for about 35 minutes, until a little risen and looking dry. Allow to cool, then slice into ½-inch-thick slices using a serrated knife.

5. Preheat the oven again to 300°F (150°C). Lay the slices out on the baking sheet (you can use the same one you baked the loaf on) and bake for 25 minutes, or until dried out, turning halfway through. Allow to cool, or enjoy warm.

Something has happened!

A passing **PURPLE DRAIK** flutters by and says, "In Neopia, Illusen Day is celebrated on the 17th of the Month of Running. On Earth, that means March 17!"

MUTANT PANCAKES

Prep time: 15 minutes • Cooking time: 20 minutes • Makes 4 servings

Mutant Neopets are, well, mutant. A **Mutant Quiggle,** for example, gains a third eye and purple skin, and a **Mutant Jetsam** proudly sports six tails. Neopets can transform into mutants by being zapped by the **Secret Laboratory Ray** or by drinking a **Transmogrification Potion.** While we generally don't recommend eating mutant food, these **Mutant Pancakes** pack a punch, and topped with blueberries? Well, that's basically a Healthy Food.

"Looks like someone spilled a Transmogrification Potion in The Bakery!"

INGREDIENTS

FOR THE PANCAKES:

1 cup (4½ oz./130g) all-purpose flour

1 teaspoon baking powder

2 tablespoons granulated sugar

Pinch of salt

1 large egg

Scant ½ cup (3½ fl. oz./100ml) whole milk

3½ tablespoons (1¾ oz./50g) butter, melted, plus extra for greasing

Green food coloring

Purple food coloring

Blueberries, to serve

FOR THE GREEN SYRUP:

¾ cup (5 oz./150g) granulated sugar

2½ tablespoons (1½ oz./40g) butter

2 tablespoons heavy cream

1 tablespoon vanilla bean paste

Green food coloring

1. Preheat the oven to 200°F (100°C).

2. Sift the flour and baking powder into a large mixing bowl. Add the sugar and salt and make a well in the middle.

3. Crack the egg in a bowl and beat the egg, then beat in the milk and butter.

4. Pour the wet ingredients into the well in the flour and begin to whisk the liquid, incorporating more and more flour from the outside of the bowl until everything is well mixed and you have a smooth, lump-free batter.

5. Ladle half of the batter into another bowl or jug. Dye one batch of batter green and the other one purple, and leave to rest while you make the sauce.

6. For the syrup, place the sugar in a saucepan with 6 tablespoons of water and set over low-medium heat. Stir until the sugar is dissolved, then cook for about 8 minutes, or until it starts to thicken to a light syrup. Turn off the heat and stir in the butter and cream. It will sizzle and bubble a bit, but keep stirring; it will become smooth. Now, stir in the vanilla and enough green food coloring to tint the mixture a mutant slime shade. Return to the heat and cook gently until warmed through again.

7. Wipe the base of a large nonstick crepe pan or frying pan with a piece of paper towel dipped in melted butter and heat it up over medium-high heat. Ladle in dollops of the batter to make 2 to 3 pancakes, depending on the size of your pan. Cook for 1 to 2 minutes, then flip over and cook for about 30 seconds on the other side, or until puffed and cooked through. Transfer to a plate, cover, and keep warm in the oven while you cook the remaining batter—both colors.

8. Pile up your pancakes in one large stack on a serving plate and drizzle over the mutant slime. Sprinkle with blueberries and serve with the remaining syrup on the side.

HEE HEE HEE!

KIND TIP!

To make this recipe dairy-free, simply swap butter, milk, and cream for your favourite nondairy versions (I suggest coconut-based for this one).

To make it vegan, do the same, and add a flax egg (1 tablespoon of ground flax combined with 2 ½ tablespoons of water, leave to sit for 5 minutes, and use like a regular egg). Just be sure the food colouring you use is plant-based too.

CHOCOLATE OMELETTE

Prep time: 10 minutes • **Cooking time:** 10 minutes • **Makes 1 omelette**

You didn't think we'd forget about the **Chocolate Omelette**, did you? This delectable omelette is quite sweet–it's topped with chocolate, after all! And better yet, you can even serve it in thirds.

"This omelette is perfect for anyone who loves chocolate. It has a chocolate topping and chocolate mixed in with the egg!"

INGREDIENTS

FOR THE OMELETTE:

1 tablespoon cocoa powder

1 tablespoon sugar

½ teaspoon vanilla extract

2 tablespoons whole milk

3 large eggs

Pinch of salt

1 tablespoon butter

FOR THE TOPPING:

2 ounces (60g) milk chocolate

1 tablespoon (15g) butter

1 tablespoon milk

1. First, get the topping going. Heat a little water in a saucepan or double boiler over medium-low heat. Place the chocolate, butter, and milk in a heatproof bowl, set the bowl over the pan, and leave to melt the mixture together, stirring occasionally, while you make the omelette.

2. In a bowl, combine the cocoa powder, sugar, vanilla extract, and milk. Whisk together until the cocoa powder is incorporated and no dry patches remain. Crack in the eggs and whisk everything together, adding a pinch of salt.

3. Heat a small, nonstick, heavy-based skillet over medium heat and add the butter. Once the pan is hot and the butter has melted, pour the egg mixture into the pan. Move it around the base a little, stirring it up with a fork as you would a normal omelette, so uncooked egg runs into the holes and cooks.

4. Once the bottom is cooked but it's still a little runny on top, shake the pan to shuffle the omelette so one edge comes up the side of the pan. Use a spatula to flip that side over the top. Then shuffle the omelette to the other side of the pan and flip the oppposite edge over, so it's folded into thirds.

5. Flip the omelette out onto a plate, pour the chocolate topping over the top, and serve immediately.

Some Neopets can be painted Chocolate too. Visit me at the Rainbow Fountain and you'll see!

TEMPLATES

Here are some handy templates to use as you cook your way through Neopia!

BAKED FAERIE CORN

(Page 32)

THESE ARE SO HELPFUL!

YURBLE POT PIE

(Page 46)

TEMPLATES

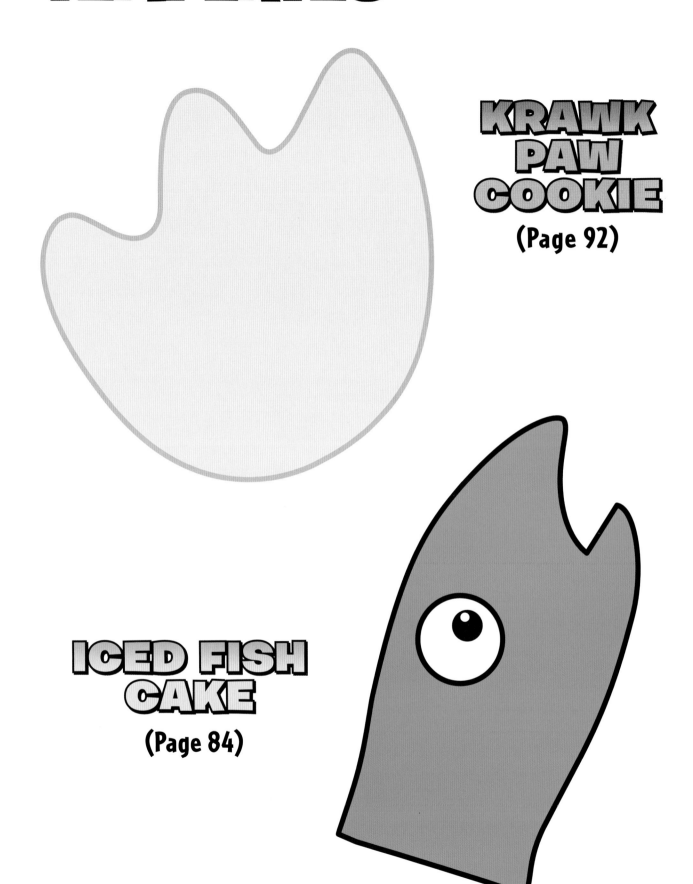

KRAWK PAW COOKIE

(Page 92)

ICED FISH CAKE

(Page 84)

PIRATE SHIP DEVILED EGGS

(Page 40)

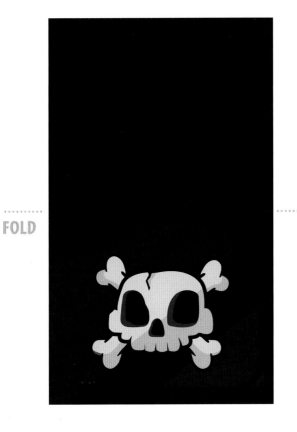

FOLD

FOLD

MERIDELLIAN-STYLE MASHED POTATOES

(Page 36)

FOLD

INDEX

INDEX

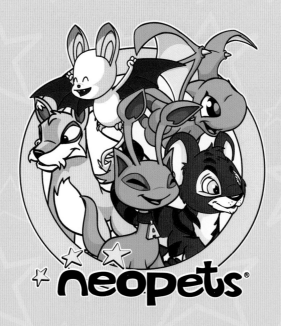

Andrews McMeel Publishing
a division of Andrews McMeel Universal
1130 Walnut Street, Kansas City, Missouri 64106

www.andrewsmcmeel.com

23 24 25 26 27 SDB 10 9 8 7 6 5 4 3 2 1

ISBN: 978-1-5248-7757-6

Library of Congress Control Number: 2022947283

Project Management and Design: Amazing 15
Writer and Food Styling: Rebecca Woods
Additional Writing: Erinn Pascal
Photography: Dan Scudamore

Editor: Erinn Pascal
Art Director: Holly Swayne
Production Editor: Elizabeth A. Garcia
Production Manager: Shona Burns

Special thanks to Colleen Gilday, Carlin West, Dean Ravenola, and Riley Swift

Use the code NEOPETSCOOKBOOK at Grundo Warehouse on neopets.com for an exclusive cookbook bonus!